Edwin J. Houston, Arthur E. Kennelly

The electric Motor and the transmission Power

Edwin J. Houston, Arthur E. Kennelly

The electric Motor and the transmission Power

ISBN/EAN: 9783743332287

Manufactured in Europe, USA, Canada, Australia, Japa

Cover: Foto ©ninafisch / pixelio.de

Manufactured and distributed by brebook publishing software
(www.brebook.com)

Edwin J. Houston, Arthur E. Kennelly

The electric Motor and the transmission Power

BY THE SAME AUTHORS

Elementary Electro-Technical Series

COMPRISING

Alternating Electric Currents.
Electric Heating.
Electromagnetism.
Electricity in Electro-Therapeutics.
Electric Arc Lighting.
Electric Incandescent Lighting.
Electric Motors.
Electric Street Railways.
Electric Telephony.
Electric Telegraphy.

Cloth,   Price per Volume, $1.00.

Electro-Dynamic Machinery.
Cloth, $2.50.

THE W. J. JOHNSTON COMPANY
253 Broadway, New York

ELEMENTARY ELECTRO-TECHNICAL SERIES

THE ELECTRIC MOTOR

AND THE

TRANSMISSION OF POWER

BY
EDWIN J. HOUSTON, Ph. D.
AND
A. E. KENNELLY, Sc. D.

NEW YORK
THE W. J. JOHNSTON COMPANY
253 BROADWAY
1896

COPYRIGHT, 1896, BY
THE W. J. JOHNSTON COMPANY.

PREFACE.

THERE is probably no subject, connected with the application of electricity, that has come into greater prominence during the last decade, than the electric transmission of power. The electric motor is now to be found everywhere driving machinery of all sizes. It permits a single, large, economical engine to operate a number of small motors over a large area.

This little volume of the *Electro-Technical Series* has been prepared with the object of rendering the principles of electric motors clear to those who are not specially trained in electro-technics. For this reason, in this, as in all other books of the series, vexed questions as regards the priority of invention have been carefully avoided, and facts, rather than names, have been presented to the reader. Only such portions of the history of the subject as are necessary to a logical comprehension of its development are given, and no mathematical treatment other than simple arithmetic has been employed.

The authors are indebted to the editors of *Cassier's Magazine* for cuts in the book relating to the Niagara power transmission.

Notwithstanding the apparent complexity of the electric motor, the authors believe that the student will be in possession of all its essential elementary principles after reading this book.

August, 1896.

CONTENTS.

CHAPTER	PAGE
I. Introductory,	1
II. Sources of Energy,	19
III. Elementary Electrical Principles,	29
IV. Early History of the Electromagnetic Motor,	73
V. Elementary Theory of the Motor,	119
VI. Structure and Classification of Motors,	162
VII. Installation and Operation of Motors,	200
VIII. Electric Transmission of Power,	217
IX. Alternating-Current Motors,	241

CHAPTER		PAGE
X.	ROTATING MAGNETIC FIELDS,	284
XI.	ALTERNATING-CURRENT TRANSMISSIONS,	302
XII.	MISCELLANEOUS APPLICATIONS OF ELECTRIC MOTORS,	335
INDEX,		359

THE ELECTRIC MOTOR AND THE TRANSMISSION OF POWER.

CHAPTER I.

INTRODUCTORY.

THE nineteenth century owes its prominence in physical science, largely to the discovery that energy is indestructible, and that the universe possesses a certain stock or store of energy which it is impossible either to increase or to decrease.

All natural phenomena are attended by transformations of energy. When energy disappears in one form, the nineteenth century doctrine of the *conservation of energy*, bids us look for some other form in which we know it must reappear. The fact that phenomena occur at one point of space where the energy necessary for this causation did not previously exist, proves that energy must have been taken from some store or stock and transmitted to that point. Consequently, the doctrine of the conservation of energy necessitates the doctrine of the transference or transmission of energy, in contradistinction to its creation. In other words, the discovery of the *indestructibility of energy* was also the discovery of the possibility of its transmission.

The discovery of the doctrine of the indestructibility and increatability of energy followed upon the discovery of the indestructibility and increatability of matter. Our belief in these doctrines is the result of our universal experience, and any explanation of natural phenomena, that necessitates the creation, either of energy or of matter, may be unhesitatingly rejected.

Energy is the capability of doing work. In other words, when work is done energy is expended. But it must not be supposed because the energy is expended, that it is thereby destroyed. The energy has only changed its form or its position. For example, when a charge of gunpowder is placed in a gun and fired, the energy which previously existed in the gunpowder is liberated, by the act of firing, and is principally expended in moving the ball from the gun, some being accidentally expended in heating the gun. Although the energy is thus properly spoken of as being expended by the gunpowder in doing this work, yet it must be remembered that the energy is not thereby annihilated, but is merely transformed. The moving ball expends some of its energy of motion in moving aside the air; a part is expended in producing sound, and the remainder, usually the greater part, is given up in the concussion against the body it strikes. All this energy finally takes the form of heat in the gun, in the air, and in the body struck, in which form it usually permanently remains. Consequently, after the gun has been fired, there is less chemical, but more heat energy in that part of the universe.

As another example take the case of a reservoir filled by a pump with water. The filled reservoir represents a stock or store of energy derived from the work expended in pumping. So long as no water is allowed to leave the reservoir, no work is done, and the store of energy remains unchanged. If, however, the water be permitted to escape through a water-wheel, the energy in the reservoir is expended in turning the wheel; that is to say, the energy of the moving water is transferred to the moving wheel, which in its turn, may transfer it to machinery connected therewith. Here each moving part expends its energy; but such energy is not annihilated; it is merely transferred. If the water-wheel were employed to drive another pump which filled a similar reservoir to the same level, and no loss of energy occurred in its transference, the escape of water from the first reservoir would result in the filling of the second reservoir with the same quantity of water and to the same depth. In practice, this never occurs; losses always take place in the machinery. Such losses, however, are not annihilations of energy. The energy which disappears, takes some other form, generally as heat produced by frictions.

The water of a river flowing through its channel, represents a stock of energy that is being expended at a certain rate. The amount of energy present in the moving stream depends both upon the quantity of water, and on the speed with which it moves. A certain proportion of this energy is capable of being transferred from the stream to a moving water-wheel, or water motor, and the water, which has passed through the wheel or motor, loses some of its motion in consequence.

The source of energy in the moving water of a river is to be found in the sun's

THE TRANSMISSION OF POWER. 7

heat, which converted the ocean's water into vapor, and carried this vapor over the land, where it subsequently condensed and fell as rain. The energy in the moving water, however, is only a portion of that which it acquired in falling from the higher to the lower level.

In each of the preceding cases the moving machinery ceased its motion, when energy ceased to be transferred to it; and, in each case, we have been able readily to trace the source of the driving energy. The case of a man, who expends muscular or nervous energy, in doing work, forms no exception to this rule. In order to permit the man to continue expending energy in such work, it is necessary that his stock of energy be replenished from time to time; in other words, that energy be transferred to him from some other source. This is accomplished by his assimilating food, which contains chemical energy imparted to it from the sun.

Strange as it may seem, the transference of energy from assimilated food to the organism of the man, is similar to the transference of energy from a lump of coal to a steam engine. The chemical potential energy of the coal, liberated by burning under a boiler, is transferred to the steam; and the energy of the steam, is transferred to the working parts of the steam engine. In man, it is the chemical potential energy of the food assimilated, which enables him to perform his varied functions. In the steam engine it is the chemical potential energy of the coal which enables it to work.

Before leaving the subject of energy it

will be advisable to obtain definite ideas concerning its measurement. The amount of energy required to be expended in order to raise one pound against the earth's gravitational force, through a vertical distance of one foot, is called a foot-pound. Thus, to raise a steel fire-proof safe, weighing 5,000 pounds, from the street to a room, 100 feet above the street level, requires the expenditure of energy equal to $100 \times 5{,}000 = 500{,}000$ foot-pounds. Energy is measurable in *units of work*, and the *foot-pound* is the unit frequently employed in English-speaking countries for this purpose.

The *international unit of work* is called the *joule*. A joule is approximately 0.738 foot-pound, and is, therefore, roughly, equal to the amount of energy required to be expended in order to raise a pound through a distance of 9″, against gravitational force. A foot-pound, is, therefore, greater than a joule, being, approximately, equal to 1.355 joules.

If we could compute the total energy of the universe, it would, of course, be capable of being expressed either in foot-pounds or in joules. As we have already stated this total is believed to be constant, all so-called expenditures of energy merely altering the character of the stock, and not its amount.

It is necessary carefully to distinguish between the expenditure of energy and the rate at which it is expended. Thus if a man weighing 150 pounds ascends a flight of stairs 100 feet high, he must necessarily expend energy amounting to $150 \times 100 = 15,000$ foot-pounds. So far as the result is concerned, namely his reaching the top of the stairs, the same amount of work must be done whether he does this in five minutes, or in one minute; but the rate at which he requires to expend energy in the two cases in order to mount the stairs, would be very different; for, in the first case he would expend 15,000 foot-pounds of work in five minutes, or at an average rate of 3,000 foot-pounds per minute, while in the second case he would expend 15,000 foot-pounds of work in one minute, or at an average rate of 15,000 foot-pounds per minute; that is to say, his *activity*, or *rate-of-expending-energy*, would be five times greater in the latter case than in the former.

A *unit of activity* or rate-of-expending-energy, frequently adopted in English-speaking countries, is the *foot-pound-per-second*. A similar unit employed in dealing with machinery is called the *horsepower* and is equal to 550 foot-pounds-per-second.

The *international unit of activity* is the *joule-per-second;* or, as it is more frequently called, the *watt*. Expressed in foot-pounds-per-second, the watt is 0.738 foot-pound-per-second, so that 746 watts are equal to one horse-power. As the watt is usually too small a unit for conveniently dealing with machinery, the *kilowatt* or 1,000 watts, is generally employed. One kilowatt (KW), is, approximately, 1 1/3 horse-power (1.34 HP), *i. e.* 746 watts = 1 HP.

As we have seen, natural phenomena require an expenditure of energy to produce them. It is convenient to regard such phenomena either from the standpoint of the energy they consume, or of the activity they require to have sustained.

We can regard these phenomena as capable of being reproduced by the expenditure of the proper amount of energy. Since the chemical potential energy in a pound of coal is a definite quantity, we know that by the liberation of this energy we can produce a certain phenomenon, such, for example, as raising a weight to a given height, or in overcoming certain resistances, as in sawing a log of wood. If the same phenomenon is to be produced at some point where this energy does not exist, it is evident that this amount of energy must be transmitted from some other point.

In mills and manufactories, where different machines are to be driven, it is possible to determine the exact amount of energy required to drive them. We can, therefore, calculate the amount of steam power or water-power required to be supplied to such establishments. In actual practice, the problem presented is the determination of the most effectual and economical means whereby this amount of power may be transmitted from the point of supply to the point of delivery, where the machine has to be driven.

Various means have been adopted for the transmission of power to considerable distances. The principal of these are:
(1) Rope transmission.
(2) Pneumatic transmission.
(3) Hydraulic transmission.
(4) Electric transmission.

Rope transmission finds its most extensive use in the operation of cable cars, where it is sometimes employed for distances of several miles in a single section.

Pneumatic transmission is employed extensively in Paris, where there are about 35 miles of pneumatic mains. It is also used extensively in mining operations, and to some extent, in systems of railway signalling. When used in mining, it possesses the advantage of aiding the ventilation.

Hydraulic transmission is in fairly extensive use for distributing power in European cities where the distribution distances are not excessive.

There can be no doubt that any of the preceding systems is capable, when properly installed, of transmitting power with fair economy over considerable distances. A transmission system consists of *generators* at the transmitting end, which transform the energy supplied into a form in which it can be transmitted; *motors*, or devices at the receiving end, for transforming the energy so transmitted into the form available for use; and *connecting systems* joining the generators and motors. In considering the relative advantages of any transmission system, it is evident that account must be taken of the cost of installation of the entire system, and of the relative efficiencies of the generators and motors; or, combining these things, of the cost of delivering power. In addition to this we must consider the readiness with which the transmitted power can be transformed, and the safety with which it can be both transmitted and employed.

In contrasting the relative advantages of rope, pneumatic, and hydraulic transmission, rope transmission is often advantageous where the power has to be transmitted in the open country in bulk, but, where power has to be transmitted to a number of consumers in a city, pneumatic or hydraulic transmission possess advantages over rope transmission, especially in cases where the exigencies of the work require the direction of the motion to be frequently and abruptly changed.

While pneumatic and hydraulic transmission systems possess marked advantages in certain directions, yet electric transmission is so convenient, the efficiency of the generators and motors so high, the cost of transmission over considerable distances so comparatively low, and the flexibility with which electricity lends itself to the purposes of general distribution so marked, that electricity is already in extensive use in the United States for the transmission of power.

CHAPTER II.

SOURCES OF ENERGY.

The known sources of energy may be classified as follows: viz.,

(1) Chemical energy, as of coal and other combustibles.
(2) Water power.
(3) The earth's internal heat.
(4) The earth's motion.
(5) Solar heat.

Tracing these various sources of energy to their origin, it soon becomes evident that they are all derived from the sun as the prime source. A lump of coal, when burned, gives out, in its radiant light and heat, the solar activity of a past geological age. So also the energy of food, which when assimilated, is the source of energy in the muscles of animals, has been derived from the sun in more recent times. Wind power and water power also manifestly derive their energy from the sun.

The earth's heat is properly to be regarded as a source of power. Since the entire interior of the earth is believed to be highly heated, we evidently have in it a great storehouse of natural power, which although never yet practically employed, yet is capable of doing an enormous amount of work. Since it is generally believed, in accordance with Laplace's nebular hypothesis, that the earth and all members of the solar system once formed a part of the sun, and were disengaged from the sun's mass while in an incandescent condition, this source of heat also owes its origin to the sun.

The rotary motion of the earth may be regarded as a source of power. Without stopping to discuss the various methods which have been proposed to obtain motion from the rotation of the earth, we would point out that the only practical means for doing this is by the employment of machines driven by the tides.

It is evident, from a consideration of the above, that all the natural sources of power available to man on the earth either have been, or are being, derived from the sun, and are divisible into three great classes; namely,

(1) Solar energy imparted to the earth at the beginning of its career.

(2) Solar energy imparted to coal during past geological epochs; and,

(3) Solar energy imparted to the earth at the present time by direct radiation.

Although, as we have already seen, the total amount of energy existing in the universe is believed to be constant, yet the amount residing in the sun and in the earth, is believed to be steadily diminishing, being lost by radiation into interstellar space at a comparatively rapid rate.

A motor which receives power and transmits it to the machinery it drives is a device for transforming or transferring energy. A certain amount of energy must be expended in driving it; that is a certain amount of activity must be delivered to the machine. This activity is generally known as the *intake* of the machine. The machine, in operating, delivers to the machinery it drives a certain amount of activity which is called its *output*. The output can never exceed the intake. In point of fact, since certain losses occur in the operation of the best designed machines, the output can never even equal the intake, and, in many machines, is considerably less than the intake. The ratio of the output to the intake is called the *efficiency* of the machine.

In order to illustrate the preceding principles we may consider the following example. A line of shafting in a machine shop, is a machine for transferring energy from a source, say a steam engine, to one or more driven machines, such as lathes, saws, etc. The amount of activity delivered to the shafting by the engine may be, say 10 horse-power, or $746 \times 10 = 7,460$

watts = 7,460 joules-per-second, or 5,500 foot-pounds per second. A certain amount of this activity is expended in overcoming the friction of the shafting; *i. e.*, in heating the journals, in churning the neighboring air, in shaking the building, and in stretching the belts. The remainder of the activity is delivered to the lathes. If this total delivery or output, be 8 HP = 746 × 8 = 5,968 watts, the efficiency of the shafting will be $\frac{8}{10}$ = 80 per cent.

Again if an electric motor receives an intake of 50 horse-power, and has an output of 45 horse-power; *i. e.*, delivers 45 horse-power at its pulley, then its efficiency will be $\frac{45}{50}$ = 0.9 = 90 per cent.

In considering the amount of power

THE TRANSMISSION OF POWER.

required to be drawn from any natural source in order to perform a given amount of work, allowance must, therefore, be made for the loss in transformation. For example, it can be shown that a pound of good coal, if thoroughly burned in air, is capable of yielding a total amount of energy equal to 15,500,000 joules, or, 11,440,000 foot-pounds. Consequently, if the energy so liberated were applied to drive a steam engine, this steam engine, if burning one pound of coal per hour, would be able to raise a weight of one pound 11,440,000 feet in that time, and would, therefore, be exerting an activity of 5.778 horse-power, or 4,310 watts. In point of fact, however, the best steam engines and boilers are only capable of delivering about $\frac{8}{10}$ths of one horse-power-hour, with one pound of coal, so that the efficiency of such an engine and boiler would only be $\frac{0.8}{5.778} = 0.1385$, or 13.85 per cent., and, in fact, with the types of engine ordinarily employed, the efficiency is commonly only about 8 per cent.

This comparatively low efficiency of a steam engine and boiler is due to the combination of two very different causes. One of these lies in the working temperature, or the difference in temperature between the steam admitted to the engine and the steam leaving the engine. It is a law of nature that the amount of heat which can be mechanically realized from the liberation, during combustion, of a given quantity of chemical energy, depends upon the working temperatures. With the working temperatures which are imposed by practical considerations in the best steam engines, the efficiency due to this cause is restricted to about 25 per cent., so that if the steam engine and boiler were perfect machines, losing none of the power which was capable of being delivered to them, they could not under these circumstances have an efficiency, taken in conjunction, of more than 25 per cent. The balance of the work is uselessly expended in heating the air and water.

The second source of loss lies in the necessary imperfections of engine and boiler as machines. The above losses are due to frictions and loss of heat by conduction, convection, radiation and condensation. Retaining the same working temperature, these losses are reduced by all improvements in the engine and boiler, considered as machines for effecting transformation of energy. The efficiency of an engine and boiler, considered as receiving only the energy which is rendered available by the range of working temperature, is at the best about 56 per cent., so that the nett efficiency, reckoned from the total chemical energy of coal, in the best engines and boilers is only about $0.25 \times 0.56 = 0.14$, or 14 per cent.

CHAPTER III.

ELEMENTARY ELECTRICAL PRINCIPLES.

THE grave mistake is not infrequently made that because we are still ignorant of the real nature of electricity, we are necessarily equally ignorant of the principles controlling its action. In point of fact the engineer has to-day a more intimate knowledge of the laws of electricity, than of the laws which govern the application of steam. Since, in the study of the electric motor, a knowledge of the more important laws of electricity is necessary, it will be advisable to discuss them briefly, before proceeding further with the subject.

An *electric current*, or *electric flow*, requires for its existence a complete conducting path as represented in Fig. 1. Here

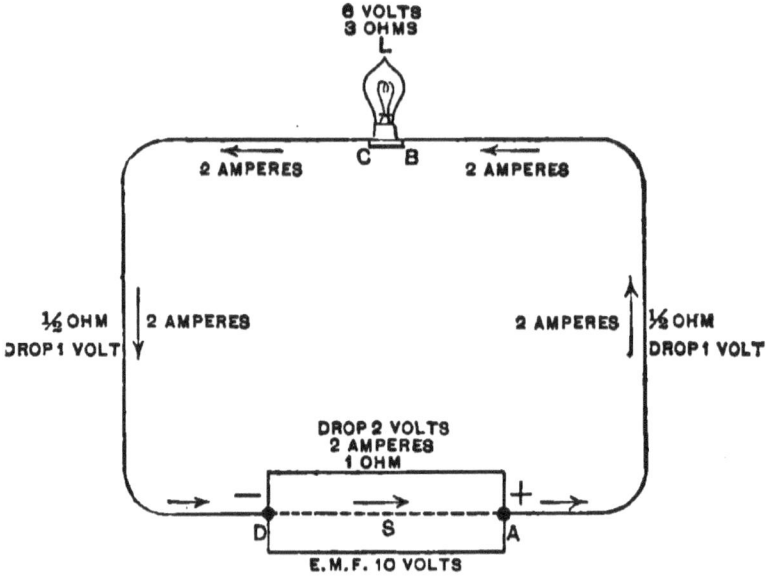

Fig. 1.—Electric Circuit, Including Source, Lamp and Conducting Leads.

a voltaic battery, or other electric source, supplies an electric current through the completed circuit, $A\ B\ C\ D$. Unless a completed path be provided for the passage of the electricity, both through the source and the external circuit, an electric current cannot be sustained. All practical electric circuits of this character consist of three separate parts; namely,

(1) The electric source.
(2) Conducting wires or leads.
(3) An electro-receptive device traversed by the current.

In all electric circuits of this type, it is convenient, for purposes of description, to regard the electricity as leaving the *source* at a point called its *positive pole*, and returning to the source, after it has passed through the circuit of the receptive devices placed therein, to a point called its *negative pole*. The current, after entering the source, flows through it and again emerges at its positive pole. It will be seen that the path thus traversed by the current is circuital, in so far as it again reaches the point from which it started. The conducting path forms what is called an *electric circuit*. It must not be supposed, however, that circuits are necessarily circular in outline, since a circuit will be established no matter what the shape of the conducting path, provided only that the electric flow reaches the point from which it is assumed to have started.

An electric circuit is said to be *made*, *completed*, or *closed*, when a complete conducting path is provided for it. It is said to be *broken*, or *opened*, when this conducting path is interrupted at any point.

When an electric source, such as shown in Fig. 1, is open or broken, the current ceases to flow, and, consequently, the source ceases to furnish electricity. It does not, however, cease to furnish a variety of force called *electromotive force*. As long as the circuit remains open the electromotive force produced by the battery does no work; *i. e.*, expends no energy. It is only when a conducting circuit is provided for it, that it can produce a motion of electricity and thus do work. In point of fact all electric sources are to be regarded as sources of *electromotive force*, usually abbreviated E. M. F., rather than sources of current, since they produce E. M. F. whether their circuit is opened or closed. Morever, the conditions of their working remaining the same, the value of their E. M. F. remains unchanged; whereas, as we shall see, the value of the current they produce, depends entirely upon certain conditions of the circuit with which they are connected.

Regarding Fig. 1, as a typical instance of a working electric circuit, provided, as already mentioned, with a voltaic battery, conducting leads, and an electro-receptive device or devices, let us inquire how we can ascertain the amount of electricity that will flow through the circuit in a given time. In this, as in any similar electric circuit, the *strength of current* which flows, that is, the quantity of electricity which passes through the circuit per second, is dependent on two quantities; namely, on the value of the E. M. F., which may, for convenience, be regarded as an *electric pressure* causing, or tending to cause, the electric flow, and on a quantity called the *resistance* of the circuit, which acts so as to limit the quantity of electricity passing through the circuit in a given time. The current strength passing is related to these quantities in a manner discovered by Dr.

Ohm, and expressed by him in a law, generally known as *Ohm's law*, as follows: The current strength in any circuit is equal to the E. M. F., acting on that circuit, divided by the resistance of the circuit.

In order to assign definite values to the above quantities, certain units are employed. The units in international use are as follows: the *unit of E. M. F.*, called the *volt;* the *unit of resistance*, called the *ohm*, and the *unit of current strength* or *flow*, called the *ampere*. Ohm's law, expressed in terms of these units, is as follows; namely,

$$\text{amperes} = \frac{\text{volts}}{\text{ohms}}.$$

Suppose, for example, in the case of the simple electric circuit shown in Fig. 1, that the E. M. F. of the voltaic battery is 10 volts, and the resistance of the entire circuit, including the resistance of the source, the conducting wires and the lamp, is 5 ohms; then, in accordance with Ohm's law, the current strength would be $\dfrac{10 \text{ volts}}{5 \text{ ohms}} = 2$ amperes.

The volt is, roughly, equal to the E. M. F. of a blue-stone voltaic cell, such as is commonly used in telegraphy. The ohm is the resistance of about two miles of ordinary trolley wire, and the ampere is about twice as strong a current as is ordinarily used in a 16 candle-power, 110-volt, incandescent lamp.

The dynamo-electric machine is the practical source of the powerful electric currents that are in common use.

Dynamos can be constructed to give an E. M. F., varying from a single volt up to 10,000 volts. The E. M. F. employed for street railroad systems is about 500 volts. The E. M. F. employed for continuous-current incandescent electric lighting is about 115 volts.

There are a great variety of voltaic cells. The value of the E. M. F. varies in each, but in general, is comprised between 2/3rds volt and 2 1/2 volts. As this pressure, or, as it is frequently called, *voltage*, is insufficient to operate most receptive devices, it is necessary to increase it by connecting a number of separate cells together so as to permit them to act as a single cell or *battery*. Such connection may be effected in various ways, but the readiest is *connection in series*, which consists essentially in connecting the positive pole of one cell to the negative of the next, and the positive of this, to the negative of the next, and so on through the entire number of cells, as

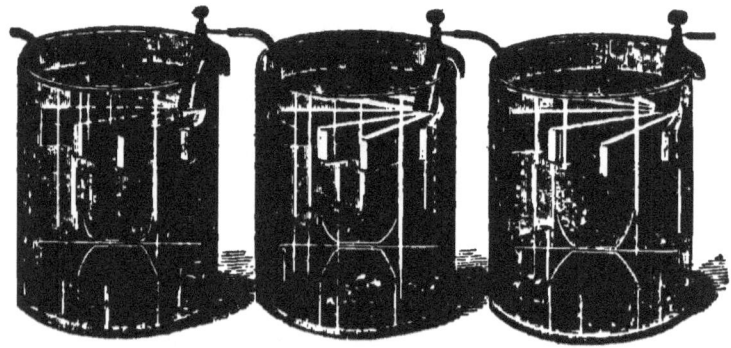

Fig. 2.—Voltaic Battery of Three Cells in Series.

shown in Fig. 2, where three separate, Daniell gravity cells are connected in series. If the E. M. F. of each cell is, say 1.1 volts, the E. M. F. of the battery will be 3.3 volts. Dynamos may also be connected in series, but since it is easy to construct a dynamo for the full E. M. F. required, the expedient is rarely resorted to.

The resistance offered by a pipe to the flow of water through it increases with the length of the pipe and also with the narrowness of its bore. A long, narrow pipe has a higher resistance, and permits less water to flow through it in a given time, and under a given pressure, than a short pipe of large diameter. In the same way, the resistance of an electric wire increases with its length and with its narrowness. A long, fine wire has a high resistance, as compared with a short, thick wire. Thus, one foot of very fine copper wire, No. 40 A. W. G. (American Wire Gauge), having a diameter of 0.003145 inch, has a resistance of, approximately, one ohm. If, therefore, the length of a wire be fixed, we can make its resistance almost anything we please by altering its area of cross-section. If we double the cross-section, we halve the resistance, the resistance increasing directly with the length, and inversely with the cross-sectional area of the wire.

There is another way of varying the resistance of wires of the same dimensions; *i. e.*, by employing different materials. In other words, the resistance of a wire depends not only upon its length and cross-section, but also upon the nature of its substance. The *specific resistance* of iron is about 6 1/2 times as great as that of copper, so that a wire of iron would have 6 1/2 times as much resistance as a wire of copper having the same length and cross-section.

In order to compare readily the specific resistances of different materials, reference is had to a quantity called the *resistivity*. The resistivity of a material is the resistance offered by a wire having unit length and unit cross-sectional area. These unit values are generally taken as one centimetre for the length, and one square centimetre for the area of cross-section, so that, when we speak of the resistivity of copper as being 1.6 microhms, we mean that a wire 1 centimetre in length and having a cross-section of 1 square centimetre, has a resistance of 1.6 *microhms;* *i. e.*, 1.6 millionths of an ohm $\left(\dfrac{1.6}{1,000,000}\right)$. The resistance of one metre of this wire would be $\dfrac{1.6 \times 100}{1} = 160$ microhms, and the resistance of one metre of a wire having a cross-sectional area of 2 square centimetres would be $\dfrac{1.6 \times 100}{2} = 80$ microhms. Consequently, if the resistivity of a material is known, it is easy to determine what the resistance of any uniform wire will be of given length and cross-sectional area.

In English-speaking countries, where lengths are generally measured in feet, and the diameters of wires in inches, it is convenient to employ as an area of cross-section the *circular mil*. A *mil* is a unit of length of the value of one thousandth of an inch, and a wire, one inch in diameter, is said to have a diameter of 1,000 mils. If we square the diameter of a wire in mils, we obtain its area in circular mils, so that a circular wire, one inch in diameter, has an area of one million *circular mils*, A *circular mil-foot* is a unit of cross-section and length possessed by a wire one foot long and having a diameter of one mil, and, consequently, an area of one circular mil. A circular mil-foot of copper has a resistance of 10.35 ohms, at 20° C.;

so that if a wire be one mile long, and have a diameter of 0.2 inch, its cross-section will be 200 × 200 = 40,000 circular mils, and its length will be 5,280 feet, so that its resistance will be $\dfrac{5{,}280 \times 10.35}{40{,}000} =$ 1.366 ohms at 20° C.

The resistivity of all metals is increased by an increase in temperature. In most metals this increase is about 0.4 per cent. per degree Centigrade, reckoned from the resistivity at zero Centigrade, so that, at the temperature of boiling water, the resistivity of copper is about 40 per cent. greater than its resistivity at the freezing point of water. In computing the resistance of a wire, therefore, its temperature must be taken into account.

When a current of water flows through a pipe, the quantity of water which passes depends both on the flow, and on the time during which the flow takes place. In the same way the quantity of electricity which passes through a wire depends both on the rate of flow, or the number of amperes, and on the time during which the flow takes place. In determining the quantity of water which passes through a pipe, the gallon is frequently employed as a unit of quantity. Similarly, in determining the quantity of electricity which passes through a wire, a *unit of electric quantity* called the *coulomb* is employed. As in water currents, the gallon-per-second might be employed as the unit of current, so in the electric current, the *unit-rate-of-flow* is taken as a *coulomb-per-second*, a rate of flow the same as the ampere already referred to. The coulomb is, therefore, the quantity of electricity which passes through a circuit

THE TRANSMISSION OF POWER. 45

during one second, when the current strength is one ampere. Thus, again referring to the simple electric circuit shown in Fig. 1, the value of the current flowing through which was calculated as two amperes, the quantity of electricity would be two coulombs in each second, or 120 coulombs per minute.

A reservoir filled with water may be regarded as a store of energy and can be caused to expend that energy in doing work, by permitting the water to escape so as to drive a water motor. The amount of energy, which can be transferred from the reservoir to the motor, will depend both on the quantity of water in the reservoir, and on the vertical height through which the water is permitted to fall. Thus, if the reservoir contain 1,000,000 pounds of water, and this drives a

E. M. F. of 10 volts is active. This pressure corresponds to the total difference of level between the water in the reservoir and the motor which it drives. Every coulomb of electricity which flows through this circuit requires an expenditure of work equal to 10 volts × 1 coulomb = 10 volt-coulombs = 10 joules = 7.38 foot-pounds. Since, as we have seen, the current strength in this circuit is 2 amperes; *i. e.*, 2 coulombs-per-second, the work done will be 2 × 10 = 20 joules in each second. A joule-per-second is called a *watt;* consequently, the activity in this circuit will be 20 watts. In any electric circuit the rate at which work is being expended; *i. e.*, the *activity* of the circuit, expressed in watts, is equal to the product of the total pressure in volts multiplied by the current strength in amperes.

THE TRANSMISSION OF POWER. 49

This activity has to be supplied to the circuit by the electric source. In the case of a dynamo, the activity is supplied by the engine or turbine driving the dynamo. In the case of a battery, the activity is supplied by the chemical energy of the cell, in other words, by the burning of the zinc in the battery solution.

The activity so expended in an electric circuit appears in one of three ways:
(1) Heat.
(2) Mechanical work.
(3) Electro-chemical work.

The relative expenditure of activity in these three different ways is determined by the distribution of what is called the *counter E. M. F.*, abbreviated C. E. M. F. For example, in Fig. 1, an E. M. F. of 10 volts acting in the circuit is opposed by

E. M. F. of 10 volts is active. This pressure corresponds to the total difference of level between the water in the reservoir and the motor which it drives. Every coulomb of electricity which flows through this circuit requires an expenditure of work equal to 10 volts × 1 coulomb = 10 volt-coulombs = 10 joules = 7.38 foot-pounds. Since, as we have seen, the current strength in this circuit is 2 amperes; *i. e.*, 2 coulombs-per-second, the work done will be 2 × 10 = 20 joules in each second. A joule-per-second is called a *watt;* consequently, the activity in this circuit will be 20 watts. In any electric circuit the rate at which work is being expended; *i. e.*, the *activity* of the circuit, expressed in watts, is equal to the product of the total pressure in volts multiplied by the current strength in amperes.

This activity has to be supplied to the circuit by the electric source. In the case of a dynamo, the activity is supplied by the engine or turbine driving the dynamo. In the case of a battery, the activity is supplied by the chemical energy of the cell, in other words, by the burning of the zinc in the battery solution.

The activity so expended in an electric circuit appears in one of three ways:
(1) Heat.
(2) Mechanical work.
(3) Electro-chemical work.

The relative expenditure of activity in these three different ways is determined by the distribution of what is called the *counter E. M. F.*, abbreviated C. E. M. F. For example, in Fig. 1, an E. M. F. of 10 volts acting in the circuit is opposed by a C. E. M. F.; *i. e.*, a *back pressure*, or oppositely directed E. M. F. opposing the flow of the current.

The passage of water through a pipe is always attended by a back pressure. For example, if a powerful stream of water be forced through a long hose, there will be a difference of pressure between the two ends of the hose, owing to the resistance encountered by the water during the passage. If the water escapes freely from the distant end into the air, the pressure in the hose, at a distance of say two hundred feet from the end, may be, perhaps, five pounds per square inch above the pressure of the air. This is the back pressure due to the flow of water. It increases with the rapidity of the discharge.

In an electric conductor or circuit, the

product of the current strength in amperes and the resistance in ohms, gives the back pressure, or C. E. M. F. in volts. Thus in the circuit of Fig. 1, where the resistance of the entire circuit is 5 ohms, and the current 2 amperes, the C. E. M. F. is $2 \times 5 = 10$ volts, which is equal to the driving E. M. F. This, in fact, follows from a consideration of Ohm's law; namely, that the E. M. F. divided by the resistance gives the current strength, so that the current strength multiplied by the resistance, is equal to the E. M. F.

Since the resistance of the circuit, shown in Fig. 1, is made up of the resistance of the voltaic battery, the conducting wires and the lamp, the C. E. M. F. or fall of pressure of 10 volts, is distributed in these portions according to their respective resistances. If the resistance of the battery be 1 ohm, that is, if the battery considered as an electric conductor composed of liquids and metals, offered a resistance of 1 ohm to the passage of the current it generates, the C. E. M. F. set up in the battery by the current strength of 2 amperes will be 2 amperes × 1 ohm = 2 volts. Or, regarded from the standpoint of Ohm's law, 2 volts will be the E. M. F. necessary to force 2 amperes through the resistance of the battery. As it is usually expressed, the "*drop*," or *fall of pressure* in the resistance of the battery will be 2 volts. Again, if the resistance of the conducting wires leading to the lamp; *i. e.*, the *leads*, be 1 ohm, or 1/2 an ohm in each conductor, the drop in each will be 2 amperes × 1/2 ohm = 1 volt. Since the resistance of the lamp is 3 ohms, the C. E. M. F., or drop in its resistance, will also be 2 amperes × 3 ohms =

6 volts. The total drop, or C. E. M. F. due to resistance, will, therefore, be 6 volts in the lamp, 2 volts in the conducting wires, and 2 volts in the battery, making the total C. E. M. F. equal and opposite to the driving E. M. F.; namely 10 volts.

As we have seen, the activity expended by a source is the product of the driving pressure or E. M. F. in that source, and the current strength in the circuit expressed in coulombs-per-second, or amperes. Similarly, the activity in watts, expended on a source of C. E. M. F., is the product of that C. E. M. F. in volts, and the current strength passing through the circuit. Thus, the activity expended in the lamp of Fig. 1, will be 6 volts × 2 amperes = 12 watts, or 8.856 foot-pounds-per-second, expended in the lamp as heat. Again, the activity expended in the two conductors is

2 volts × 2 amperes = 4 watts, or 2.952 foot-pounds-per-second. The activity expended in the internal resistance of the battery will be also 2 volts × 2 amperes = 4 watts = 2.952 foot-pounds-per-second, while the activity expended in the entire circuit of the battery will be 10 volts × 2 amperes = 20 watts = 15.76 foot-pounds-per-second.

Summing up the various activities in the circuit, we have, as follows; viz.,

The activity expended on the circuit by the source is 10 volts × 2 amperes = 20 watts = 20 joules-per-second. Of this the activity expended in the circuit by the lamp is 6 volts × 2 amperes = 12 watts; the activity expended in the two leads, is 2 volts × 2 amperes = 4 watts; the activity expended in the battery, is 2 volts × 2 amperes = 4 watts; total activity = 20 watts.

In the above case the activity is expended by the chemical energy in the battery, and is liberated entirely in the form of heat; that is to say, the battery is warmed, the wires are warmed, and the lamp is warmed. The lamp becomes much hotter than either the battery or the wires, because the heat is liberated in a very small volume of material, and can escape only from a very contracted surface. All activity expended against the C. E. M. F. of drop is *thermal activity* and is usually to be considered as *wasted activity*, except in the case of electric heaters or electric lamps, where this C. E. M. F. and activity are designedly employed for warming the surrounding air or other bodies.

When an electric motor is so placed in any circuit, that a current passes through it, there will be produced in it a drop or C. E. M. F. due to resistance only; provided that the motor be prevented from moving. If, however, the motor be driven by the

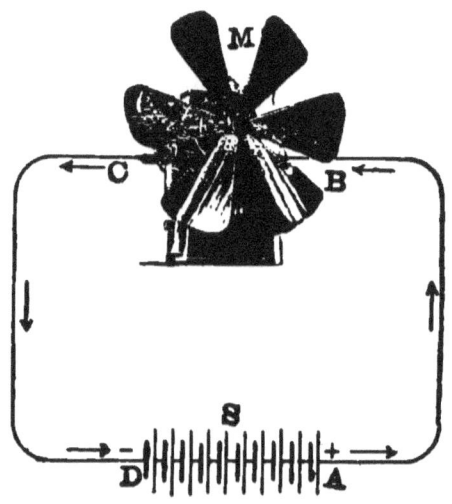

Fig. 3.—Electric Circuit Containing Source, Leads and Motor.

current, then there is produced an additional C. E. M. F. which is generated by the rotation of the motor. Thus, if the motor *M*, in Fig. 3, has a resistance of 1 ohm, and the leads to the motor have each a resistance of 1 ohm, while the internal resistance of the battery or electric source is also 1 ohm, then the total resistance of the circuit will be 4 ohms, and, as long as the motor is prevented from running, the current strength in the circuit will be 10 volts divided by 4 ohms = 2.5 amperes. The activity expended by the source will, therefore, be 10 volts × 2.5 amperes = 25 watts, and this activity will be entirely expended in heating the circuit. 6 1/4 watts will be expended in warming the battery, 6 1/4 watts in warming each wire, and 6 1/4 watts in warming the wire wound upon the motor.

If, however, the motor be permitted to run, and, therefore, to do work, it must expend energy; and this expenditure must be supplied from the circuit as the product of a C. E. M. F. and the current strength which it opposes. Thus, if the motor by its rotation generates a C. E. M. F. of 2 volts, in addition to its C. E. M. F. of drop, the E. M. F. acting on the circuit will be 10 volts in the battery, less 2 volts C. E. M. F. of rotation produced by the motor, or 8 volts, as the resultant driving E. M. F., capable of being expended in forcing current through the circuit against resistance. The current strength will, therefore, be 8 volts ÷ 4 ohms = 2 amperes, and the activity of the source will be 10 volts × 2 amperes = 20 watts = 14.76 foot-pounds. The drop in the battery will be 2 amperes × 1 ohm = 2 volts; that in each of the leads 2 volts; and that in the winding of the motor 2 volts. The total pressure at motor terminals is, therefore, 4 volts. The activity expended as heat will, therefore, be 2 volts

× 2 amperes = 4 watts in the battery, 4 in each of the wires, and 4 in the motor winding = 16 watts in all. The activity in the motor available for mechanical work, is, however, the C. E. M. F. of rotation, or 2 volts × 2 amperes = 4 watts, so that the total amount of work which the motor can perform mechanically is 4 watts, or 2.952 foot-pounds-per-second. It is to be observed, therefore, that while 20 watts are expended by the source, only 4 watts can in this instance be utilized for mechanical purposes, the balance being expended in heating the circuit.

Analyzing the activity in the circuit we have: Total activity of battery 10 volts × 2 amperes = 20 watts = 14.76 foot-pounds-per-second. This must be expended in the circuit as a whole. The drop, or C. E. M. F. due to resistance in the two leads, is 4 volts, so that the activity in warming the leads is 4 volts × 2 amperes = 8 watts. The drop in the battery is 2 volts, so that the activity in warming the battery is 2 volts × 2 amperes = 4 watts. The drop in the motor is 2 volts; the C. E. M. F. of rotation is 2 volts; the total C. E. M. F. is 4 volts. The activity in the motor is, therefore, 4 volts × 2 amperes = 8 watts; total, 20 watts. Of the 8 watts total activity in motor, 4 watts will be expended in heating its wire, and 4 watts in producing rotation.

We have already referred to the fact that when water escapes from a reservoir through a pipe a back pressure, or a *counter watermotive force* is produced in the pipe, tending to check the flow. Fig. 4, represents a reservoir R, maintained at a practically constant level. Suppose a horizontal pipe B O, be provided with an outlet at O. If the outlet at O, be temporarily closed, then the pressure from the water in R, will cause the water to

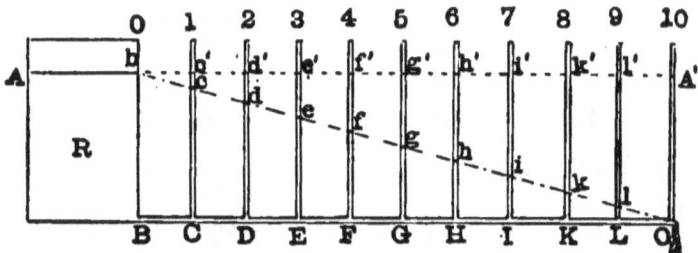

Fig. 4.—Reservoir Discharging Water Through an Outlet Pipe.

stand at the same level A A', in all the vertical pipes, 1, 2, 3, 4, etc. If, however, the outlet pipe be opened, the pressure at the outlet will fall to zero; i. e., become that of the pressure in the air, and the liquid will escape owing to the difference of pressure between this point and that in the reservoir. There will, therefore, be established a *gradient of pressure b C*, which will be practically uniform if the pipe be uniform, and the pressure in the pipe will be represented by the respective columns of water at b, c, d, e, f, etc. The back pressure at the reservoir, due to the flow of water through the pipe, is $b\,B$, or the fall of pressure in the reservoir. At 1, the back pressure is represented by the column $c\,C$, and the drop of pressure in the length $B\,C$, is represented by the column of water $c\,c'$. Similarly, the back pressure at 2, is represented by the column $d\,D$, and the drop in the length $C\,D$, by the column $d\,d'$. Similarly, the drop in the whole length $B\,O$, is $b\,B$, or $A'\,O$. In other words, the pressure $b\,B$, is that which is required to produce, through the resistance of the pipe, the actual flow which takes place through it.

If we consider a pound of water in the pipe after leaving the reservoir, then when this pound of water has reached the point 1, it has virtually fallen through the height $c\,c'$, and, therefore, the amount of work expended by the reservoir in forcing the water through the pipe against this back pressure $c\,c'$, will be this pound multiplied by the number of feet in $c\,c'$. Again, if the flow from the reservoir be say 50 pounds-per-second, then the expenditure of activity in foot-pounds-per-second, will be 50 pounds × height $O\,A'$. If this be 10 feet, the activity of the reservoir will be $50 \times 10 = 500$ foot-pounds-per-second $= 678$ watts.

The preceding principles are those, which as we have seen, apply to the electric circuit. If we represent the number of pounds of water by the coulombs, the difference of level in feet, by the volts, and the pounds-per-second, by the amperes, the analogy is complete: for, if we multiply the current flow in amperes, by the drop of pressure caused by the resistance in volts, we have the joules-per-second, or the watts of activity, expended by the electric source in order to drive the electricity through the circuit against its resistance, or against the C. E. M. F. which this resistance produces. It must be remembered, however, that electricity is not a gross liquid like water and that these are merely analogies.

Fig. 5 represents a reservoir with an outlet pipe as before, but coupled to a small water motor M, inserted in the pipe. This water motor absorbs activity by reason of the back pressure it is capable of developing when in rotation. It will be observed that the driving pressure in the reservoir is now equal to the sum of the drops of pressure in the pipe, and the back pressure of the motor M. Thus d_1, is the drop of pressure in the first section of the pipe, d_2, the

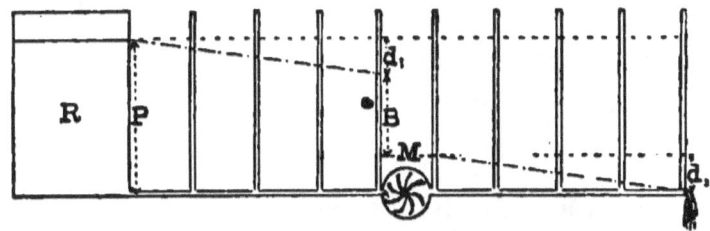

Fig. 5.—Distribution of Pressures in Motor and Pipe.

drop of pressure in the second section of the pipe, and B, is the back pressure due to the action of the motor, so that d_1, B, and d_2, are together equal to P.

The activity expended by the reservoir in forcing the water through the pipe and motor together, is equal to the flow, say 50 pounds-per-second, multiplied by the total driving head P, say 10 feet = 50 × 10 = 500 foot-pounds-per-second. Of this activity that which is expended in forcing the water through the pipe, against the drop of pressure due to its resistance, is expended in warming both the pipe and the water, while the activity expended against the back pressure B, of the motor, may be entirely employed in producing mechanical work, and would be so expended if the motor M, were a perfect machine. Thus if d_1, be 2 feet and d_2, 2 feet, while B, is 6 feet, the activity expended in heating the pipe and its contents is 4 feet × 50 pounds-per-second = 200 foot-pounds-per-second; while the activity expended in the motor is 6 feet × 50 pounds-per-second = 300 foot-pounds-per-second. Moreover, the larger the pipe, and the shorter its length, the less will be the drop for a given flow, and the greater the proportion of activity which may be expended in driving the motor.

The electric analogue is shown in Fig. 6, where the source is represented as a

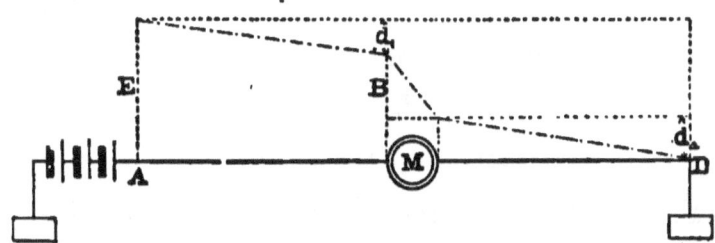

Fig. 6.—Electric Analogue Showing Distribution of Pressure in Motor and Wires.

battery or dynamo producing the E. M. F. or difference of electric level E. The circuit $A\ D$, extends from one pole of the battery to the other, although not so shown in the drawing. The motor M, produces a back pressure B, which we may assume to be entirely due to its rotation, the resistance of the motor being negligible; the resistance of the conducting wires is 2 ohms each, the drop in the conducting wires is represented by d_1, and d_2, as before, but expressed in volts instead of in feet. If the E. M. F. at generator terminals be 10 volts, d_1 and d_2, each 2 volts, and the back pressure of the motor 6 volts, then the current through the circuit will be 10 − 6 = 4 volts divided by 4 ohms = 1 ampere. The activity expended by the source will be 10 volts × 1 ampere = 10 watts = 7.38 foot-pounds-per-second. The activity expended in each of the leads will be 2 volts × 1 ampere = 2 watts, or 4 watts in all, and the balance, or 6 watts, must be equal to the activity expended in the motor; namely, 6 volts × 1 ampere. If the motor could be made perfect, it would supply 6 watts mechanically at its shaft, or 4.428 foot-pounds-per-second, available for driving purposes, and the proportion of the available activity in the circuit to the total activity expended would be $\frac{6}{10} = 60$ per cent. In practice, owing to the existence of various frictional forces in the motor, its output would be less than 6 watts, say 4, making

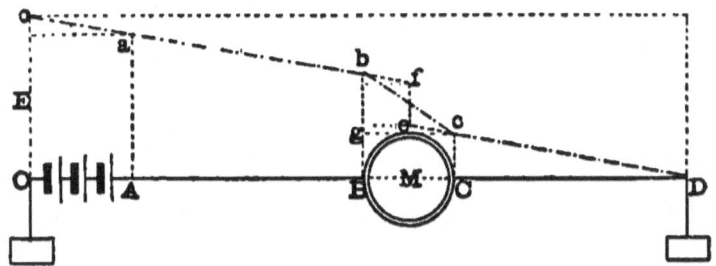

Fig. 7.—Distribution of Electric Pressure in a Circuit.

its efficiency $\frac{4}{6} = 66\ 2/3$ per cent., and the efficiency of the circuit $\frac{4}{10} = 40$ per cent.

Fig. 7 represents a more nearly complete analysis of the distribution of drop and expenditure of energy in a circuit consisting of a source, a motor and conducting wires.

The E. M. F. of the battery or source is represented by E. The resistance of the battery by the length $O\,A$, the resistance of conducting wires by the lengths $A\,B$ and $C\,D$, and the resistance of the motor by the length $B\,C$. Then, if $e\,f$, represents the back pressure of the motor due to its rotation, the pressure in the circuit will follow the line $o\,a\,b\,f\,e\,c\,D$. If $O\,o$, represents 10 volts, $O\,A$, 1 ohm, $A\,B$ and $C\,D$ 2 ohms each, $B\,C$, 1 ohm, then the total resistance of the circuit will be 6 ohms. Also, if the back pressure $e\,f$, be 4 volts, the total E. M. F. in the circuit available for producing current through resistance will be $10-4=6$ volts, so that by Ohm's law the current strength will be 6 volts divided by 6 ohms $=1$ ampere.

The activity expended in the source will be 1 watt; that in the conducting wires 4 watts; and that in the resistance of the motor 1 watt, making a total thermal activity of 6 watts, and leaving an activity of 4 watts to be expended in the motor available for purpose of producing rotation. As a matter of fact, however, the back pressure in the motor is not developed at any one spot, say halfway through its resistance, but will probably be developed uniformly through all parts of the resistance, and the combined effect of C. E. M. F. due to rotation and drop in resistance will be indicated by the dotted line $b\ c$, having a different gradient to the line $o\ b$, or $c\ D$.

It will be observed that the drop in the battery is the difference in pressure between E, and $A\ a$, or $O\ o$. The drop in the leads will be the difference in pressure between $A\,a$ and $B\,b$, and between $C\,c$ and D, respectively. The total drop in the motor will be $b\,g$, or the difference between $B\,b$ and $C\,c$. This drop is composed of two parts; namely, $e\,f$, due to rotation which would disappear when the motor came to rest, and which represents the C. E. M. F. available for useful work, and the difference between $e\,f$ and $b\,g$, which is the drop in the resistance of the motor with a current of one ampere.

CHAPTER IV.

EARLY HISTORY OF THE ELECTROMAGNETIC MOTOR.

PROBABLY one of the most valuable gifts of electromagnetic science to the industrial world is that of the electromagnetic motor. The history of this subject is not only interesting on its own account, but also affords, perhaps, the best line that can be followed in the discussion of its theory.

The electric motor, as it exists to-day, is a marvel of ingenuity. As a means for converting electrical into mechanical energy it cannot but be regarded as an exceptionally efficient piece of apparatus.

Like other great achievements, the electric motor has not been the product of any single man or nation, but is rather the embodiment of the life work of many able workers, from many countries, through many years. As Emerson has aptly expressed it: "Not in a week, or a month, or a year, but by the lives of many souls, a beautiful thing must be done."

Since the electromagnetic motor consists essentially of means whereby a continuous rotary motion is produced, by the combined agency of an electric current and a magnet, we must regard the first electric motor as being due to Faraday, who, in 1821, produced the apparatus shown in Fig. 8. Here a permanent steel bar magnet $S\,N$, is fixed in a cork, which wholly closes the lower end of a glass tube. Enough mercury is poured in to partly cover the magnet. An electric current is caused to flow in the neighborhood of the magnet, through a movable wire *a b*, so suspended as to be capable of rotat-

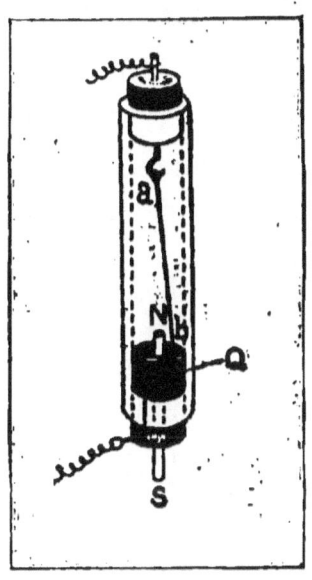

Fig. 8.—The First Electromagnetic Motor.

ing its lower extremity about the axis of the tube. Under the combined action of the current and the magnet, a continuous rotary motion is produced. The direction of this motion depends upon the direction of the current, as well as on the polarity of the magnet; that is to say, if the motion be *right-handed*, or *clockwise*, when the current is in one direction through the wire, it will be *left-handed*, or *counter-clockwise*, if the direction of current be reversed. Similarly, a reversal of the polarity of the magnet, will reverse the direction of the motion. The current passes through the conductor in the upper cork to the hook a, thence through the movable wire $a\ b$, and out, by means of the mercury and the lower conductor.

Let us inquire into the cause which produces the electromagnetic rotation in the case of the simple apparatus shown in Fig. 8. To do this, a brief examination into the elementary principles of magnetism will be necessary.

We have experimental knowledge of the fact that magnets possess the power of mutual attraction and repulsion, at sensible distances from one another. It would seem at first sight, that magnets possess the power of producing action at a distance, without the presence of any intervening mechanism, or connecting medium, but this doctrine is now totally discredited. Indeed, it can be shown that a certain influence emanates from the magnet, so that a magnet is a piece of visible matter accompanied and surrounded by an invisible influence, which must be regarded as a part of the magnet itself. Moreover, the invisible part is much larger than the visible part. This invisible part, or *magnetic field*, may be described as a region traversed by an emanation called *magnetic flux*. The existence of this flux is shown either by the action exerted upon a movable compass needle, when brought into or out of the field, or by the power it possesses to cause iron filings to align themselves in definite directions. In Fig. 9, the direction of the flux paths is shown by means of the groupings of iron filings which have been sprinkled on a glass plate placed over a bar magnet.

Regarding the grouping of filings as indicating the paths of magnetic flux, in the plane of the glass plate, it will be seen that curved chains of filings connect the two ends N, and S, of the magnet, although in the outlying portions of the figure the interconnection of these lines is not shown. We know, however, that if the figure were large enough, all the lines would be found to form complete closed paths. Moreover, it can be shown that

FIG. 9.—GROUPINGS OF IRON FILINGS SHOWING MAGNETIC FLUX LINES OF BAR MAGNET.

this flux not only occupies the space outside the magnet, but also penetrates its substance, and that, in fact, each flux path forms an endless chain, passing through both the substance of the magnet and the region outside the magnet. The question naturally arises whether the magnetic flux, or at least that part of it which lies outside the magnet, is not due to the presence of the air or other gross medium occupying this space. This, however, is not the case, since the same phenomena occur if a vacuum exists outside the magnet, that is to say, if the magnet be enclosed in a chamber exhausted by an air-pump.

There is, however, a medium called the *universal ether*, which, as can be shown, does fill this, as well as all other space. The air-pump is unable to remove this medium, since it can readily pass through the substance of glass or of any other known material. Although the exact nature of magnetic flux is unknown, yet it is convenient, for purposes of explanation, to assume that it consists of a streaming motion of the ether; the curved lines, occupied by the iron filings, corresponding to the *stream-lines* or lines in which the ether is flowing.

Since a flow necessitates a motion in a definite direction, it is conventionally assumed that the *ether streams;* i. e., the *magnetic flux*, issue from the magnet at its *north pole;* namely, the pole which would point northwards, if the magnets were freely suspended, and after having passed through the region outside, returns into the substance of the magnet at its *south pole*, then passing through the substance of the magnet and reissuing at its north pole.

In other words, a magnet may be regarded as a means for producing a streaming motion of the ether. That is to say, an ether streaming, called magnetic flux, moves in closed paths or circuits around the magnet. According to this view, a bar magnet acts relatively to the ether which permeates and surrounds it, in the same way as a tube placed in water and furnished with a pump in its interior, which causes a steady stream of water to emerge from the tube at one end, and to re-enter at the other end, after passing through the surrounding liquid.

What we call the magnetic properties of a magnet only continue to exist while the magnet is producing these streaming ether motions; that is, while it is producing magnetic flux. Anything which causes this motion to cease, causes the magnet to lose its magnetic properties, and anything which enables the magnet to again produce this flux, will enable it to regain its magnetic properties. Since a magnetized bar of hardened steel retains its magnetism for an indefinite time, we assume that it possesses the power of indefinitely producing the ether motion. This could exist without loss of energy if we assume, as we believe to be true, that ether is a frictionless fluid.

But there are other ways of setting up streaming ether motion; *i. e.*, producing magnetic flux around gross matter. If an electric conductor, say a copper wire, has an electric current passed through it, the streaming ether motion will be set up in concentric circles around it. The presence of this circular magnetic flux may be shown by groupings of iron filings ob-

84 THE ELECTRIC MOTOR AND

tained in a similar manner to that described in the case of the bar magnet and

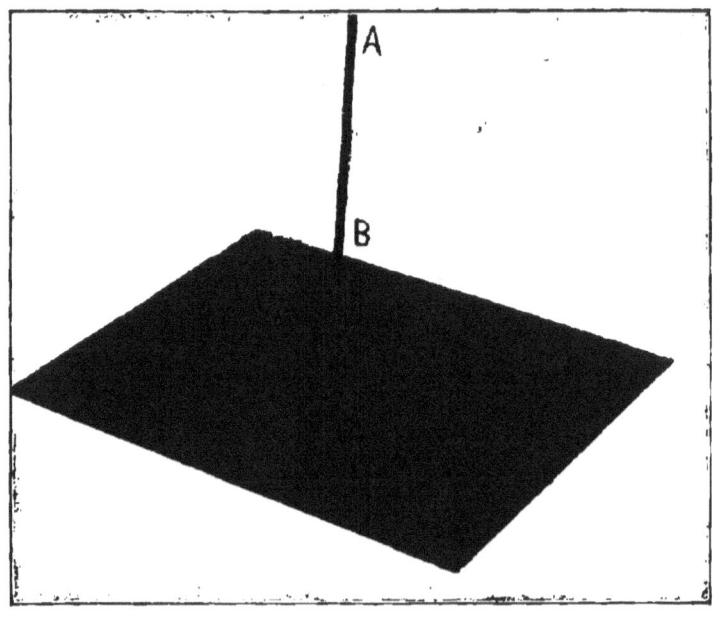

FIG. 10.—CIRCULAR DISTRIBUTION OF FLUX AROUND ACTIVE CONDUCTOR.

shown in Fig. 9. Such groupings in the case of an active wire are shown in Fig. 10. Here a horizontal sheet of paper has been placed perpendicularly to a vertical wire while an electric current is passing through it.

The circular magnetic flux, produced around an active conductor by an electric current, like the flux produced by a permanent bar magnet, has a definite direction dependent on the direction of current in the wire. If the current be considered to pass through the wire away from the observer, the magnetic streamings around the conductor will have the same direction as that of the hands of a watch, as seen by an observer facing them. Reversing the direction of the current will reverse the direction of the streamings. The streamings cease as soon as the current ceases. In other words, the magnetic flux around a wire is dependent upon the existence of the electric current.

Fig. 11, represents diagrammatically the magnetic flux passing through the north pole of a magnet into the region occupied

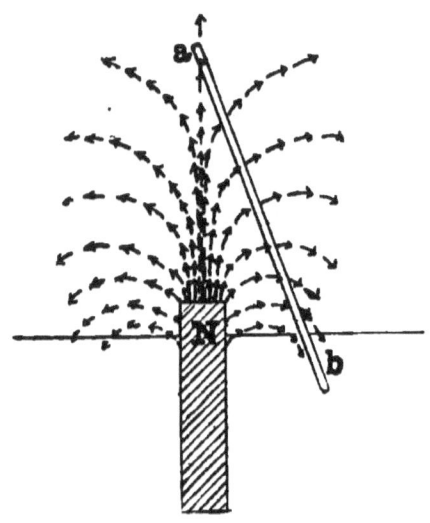

Fig. 11.—Diagrammatic Representation of Flux from Magnet, Shown in Fig. 8.

by the wire *a b*, of Fig. 8. If no current passes through the wire, this magnetic flux does not tend to produce any motion in the wire. If, however, a current passes through the wire, so that magnetic flux streams around it, then the interactions of the two magnetic fluxes produce a tendency to move the conductor across the magnetic flux from the magnet, and, consequently, cause the wire to move in a circular path around the magnetic pole. The combination, therefore, of an active conductor and an independent magnetic flux, constitutes a simple electromagnetic motor.

As is well known, action and reaction are always equal and opposite, so that if the magnet pulls the wire around it through the medium of the interacting magnetic fluxes, the wire is also producing a pull on the magnet. Consequently, if the wire be fixed and the magnet be free to move about its vertical axis, it may be made to rotate. This was actually done by Faraday, and others after him, in a variety of apparatus.

Feeble as was the early motor of Faraday represented in Fig. 8, yet it essentially embodied the principles of the most complex, powerful and efficient electromagnetic motors of to-day, and a comprehension of the principles involved in this simple motor gives the clue to the action of all modern motors.

Fig. 12, represents a modified form of the early motor shown in Fig. 8. Here the electric current passes from the base of the instrument through the vertical bar magnet A B. The metallic support D, has pivoted at its upper extremity a delicately suspended rectangular conductor E F, which has its two free ends dipping into a circular trough of mercury. The current divides through this rectangular loop, passing down through E and F. Under these circumstances, a continuous rotary motion of the rectangular circuit is produced. This apparatus only differs from the pre-

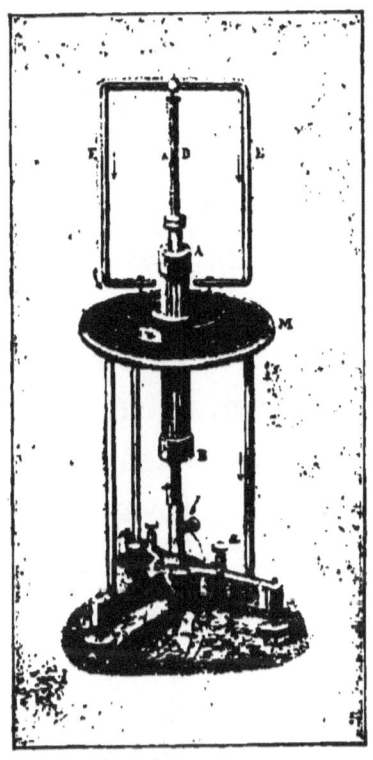

Fig. 12.—Modified Form of Faraday Motor.

ceding in the fact that two wires carry the current past the magnet, instead of one.

The fact that magnets exhibit mutual attractions and repulsions for one another, was known from the dawn of magnetic science, before the Christian era, and the idea of obtaining mechanical motion from magnets naturally originated at, perhaps, an equally early date. Continuous motion was, and still is, impossible with permanent magnets, for the reason that when a magnet has attracted either a piece of iron, or another magnet, it cannot again repel the same unless its magnetism is reversed, and no means for reversing magnetism were known, until the magnetic properties of the electric current were discovered.

Although Faraday was the first to produce a continuous electromagnetic rotation, and is justly entitled to the honor of priority, yet the principle which he adopted was that discovered by Oersted in 1819.

THE TRANSMISSION OF POWER. 91

Oersted's discovery not only showed how a magnet could be produced by an electric current, but also, for the first time in the history of science, afforded the means of reversing at will the direction of magnetism, and thus obtaining a continuous rotary motion.

Oersted showed that when an electric circuit was completed, the circuit thereby acquired magnetic properties, and possessed the power of attracting or repelling magnets brought into its vicinity, the tendency of such attraction or repulsion being to cause a magnet to set itself at right angles to the electric current. The apparatus for demonstrating this important principle consists essentially of a wire AB, carrying a current, and brought into the vicinity of a freely suspended horizontal compass needle, as shown in Fig. 13. As-

92 THE ELECTRIC MOTOR AND

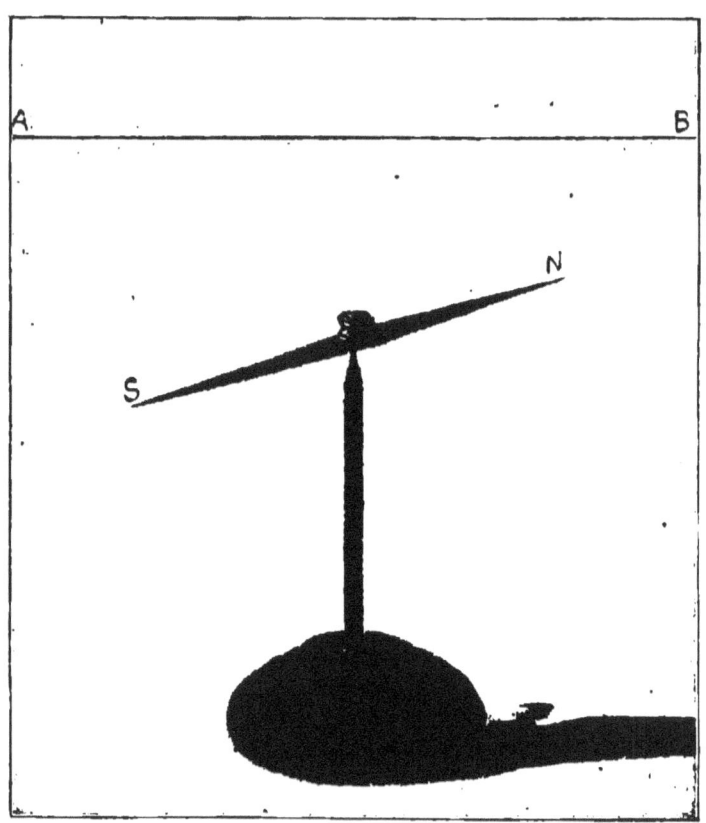

Fig. 13.—Oersted's Experiment.

suming the magnet to be placed parallel to the conductor, then as soon as the current flows through the wire, the needle will be deflected and will tend to occupy a position at right angles to the wire. On the cessation of the current in the wire, the needle returns to its original position under the influence of the earth's magnetism. The direction in which the needle is deflected will depend upon the direction of the electric current. If we reverse the direction of the current in the wire, we reverse the direction of deflection in the needle, because we reverse the direction of the magnetic flux passing around the wire. Also, if we obtained one direction of deflection when the wire is held above the needle, the opposite direction of deflection will be obtained when the wire is held beneath the needle. The cause of these phenomena is due to the mutual action of the flux produced by the needle and that produced by the current in the wire, which latter disappears on the cessation of the current.

It would be possible, by suitably changing the direction of the current, to set up a continuous rotation of the needle, and, in point of fact, the electric motor of to-day consists of means whereby the direction of the current is changed at such times as will effect the continuous rotation of the magnet.

Various devices were suggested by Faraday and others for producing continuous rotary motion by electromagnetic action. For example, in 1823, Barlow produced the apparatus shown in Fig. 14. Here an electric current passes between the centre of a star-shaped wheel and emerges at its lowest point, which dips in a trough of mercury included in the circuit.

THE TRANSMISSION OF POWER.

A horse-shoe magnet N.S. produces a magnetic flux, which acting in conjunction with the flux produced by the current

FIG. 14.—BARLOW WHEEL MOTOR.

through the star wheel, produces a continuous rotation of the latter. Here that part of the wheel lying between its axis and the point dipping into the mercury cup corresponds to the movable wire shown in Figs. 8 and 13. Instead, however, of the same wire, or wires, being continuously acted on, different portions or teeth of the star wheel are continuously acted on. As before, the direction of motion is at right angles to the magnetic flux produced between the poles of the horse-shoe.

A modification of Barlow's wheel was shortly afterward made by Sturgeon. Here a continuous disc, instead of a star wheel, was employed for the moving part.

None of the early motors, so far described, were capable of exerting much activity, but such activity as they did exert, was derived, as in the case of all electric motors, from the source supplying their driving current.

The mechanical activity developed in a motor, neglecting frictional losses, is equal to the product of the current strength in amperes, passing through the motor, and the C. E. M. F. in volts developed by the motor through its rotation. The star wheel represented in Fig. 14, produces a C. E. M. F. when it commences to turn, and to this extent the rotating motor tends to act as a dynamo-electric machine, or source of E. M. F. It is a general law, discovered by Faraday, that when an electric conductor is moved across a magnetic flux, an E. M. F. is developed in the conductor, whether a current be flowing through the conductor or not. Consequently, when the spurs of the star wheel rotate under the influence of the force produced by the mutual interaction of the fluxes of the magnet and the current, generally called the *electro-dynamic force,* the motion of the spurs through the flux produced by the magnet, establishes in the spurs an E. M. F. which is counter, or op-

FIG. 15.—FARADAY'S DISC DYNAMO.

posed, to the direction of the current in them. The product of this C. E. M. F. and the current strength, is equal to the activity developed by the wheel.

Any electric motor is, therefore, capable of acting as a dynamo, if, instead of being driven by the current, it is moved by mechanical force. In fact no electromagnetic motor can operate unless it be capable, under the circumstances, of acting as a dynamo, since, otherwise, the motor would be unable to absorb or take activity from the circuit. This fact, however, was not discovered until 1831, when Faraday produced what was, in reality, the first dynamo-electric generator designed for purposes of producing electromotive forces in this manner.

Faraday's early apparatus is represented in Fig. 15. Here a disc of copper is so mounted as to be capable of rotation between the poles of a horse-shoe magnet. Under these circumstances, E. M. F's. will be set up in the disc, between its centre and edge, and these E. M. F's. may be caused to produce a current in an external circuit by means of collectors, one connected with the axis of the disc, and the other with its periphery. The direction of these E. M. F's. will depend both on the direction of rotation of the disc and on the position of the poles of the magnet. Reversing either the polarity of the magnet, or reversing the direction of rotation, will reverse the direction of the E. M. F.; and, consequently, the direction of the current supplied to the external circuit, but it always happens that the direction of the E. M. F. which is developed in such a machine, or indeed, in any motor, when rotated by electromagnetic forces supplied by a current, is opposed or counter to the direction of the driving current.

If, therefore, instead of rotating the wheel shown in Fig. 16, it be left at rest, and an electric current from an

THE TRANSMISSION OF POWER. 101

external source be sent through it in the direction of the arrows, then, under the influence of the electro-dynamic force a

FIG. 16.—JACOBI'S ELECTRIC MOTOR.

rotation of the wheel will be produced in the opposite direction to that represented by the arrow.

Without attempting to trace fully the gradual developments of the electric motor, it suffices to say that one of the earliest practical motors was produced by Jacobi in 1834, and perfected in 1838. This motor is interesting from a historical standpoint, from the fact that in its improved form it was employed for the propulsion of a boat on the river Neva, in 1838. In this case the motor was driven by a voltaic battery.

Jacobi's electric motor is represented in Fig. 16. Here two vertical, parallel frames of wood, support a number of *horse-shoe electromagnets;* i. e., horse-shoe-shaped iron cores, wound with insulated copper wire. Such a magnet acquires its magnetism almost instantly on the passage of an electric current, and almost instantly loses it when the current ceases. It is thus capable of becoming magnetized and demagnetized with great rapidity. The magnets in the outer frame were kept permanently excited by a steady electric current from the battery. Between these frames a wooden star wheel was supported on the axis *a a*. In the spurs of this star wheel were mounted the six sets of electromagnets *s, s, s, s, s, s*. The insulated wires leading to these bar magnets were connected with the commutating apparatus *c*, in such a manner that the brushes *h, h*, resting on the commutator disc, supplied an electric current to the rotating magnets from the battery. As soon as the current was supplied to the star wheel magnets, they attracted the fixed electromagnets in their vicinity and pulled around the star wheel to meet them, but just as they came opposite to one another, the rings *C*, reversed the current passing into the moving magnets, thus permitting the magnets in the frame to repel them, and the magnets next in succession to attract them. In this way a continuous rotary motion was produced.

The first electric motor produced in the United States was that of Davenport, who in 1837, designed an electromagnetic motor in which permanent magnets, placed on a fixed frame, attracted and were attracted by electromagnets placed on a moving frame. Davenport perfected his motor to an extent which enabled him to apply it to the driving of a printing press, and to the operation of a small model of a circular railway, which he exhibited at Springfield, Mass.

The principal of the operation of the Jacobi motor may, perhaps, be better un-

THE TRANSMISSION OF POWER. 105

derstood by an examination of a motor designed by Ritchie, which operates on the

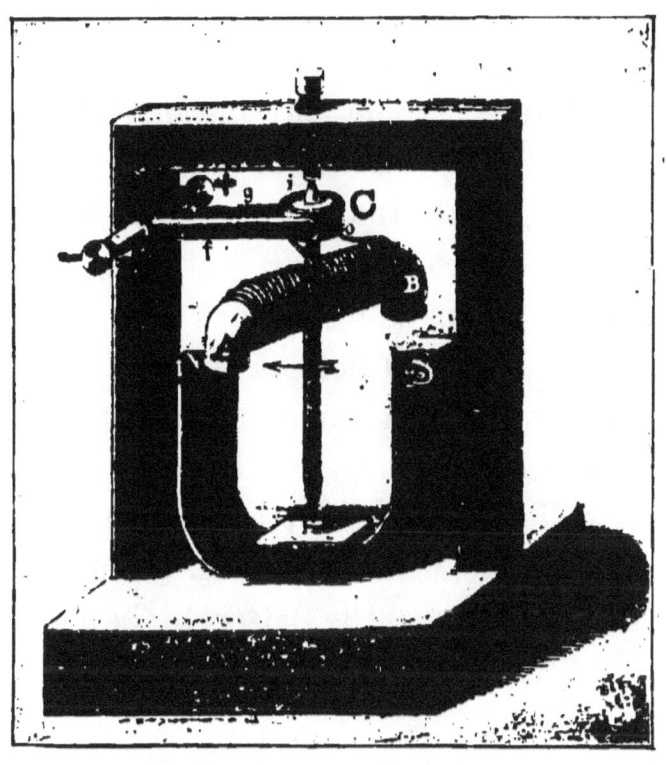

Fig. 17.—Ritchie's Motor.

preceding principles. Ritchie's motor is shown in Fig. 17. Here a movable electromagnet A B, is caused to continuously rotate under the mutual interaction of its flux and the flux produced by a permanent magnet N S. Suppose the electromagnet to occupy at any instant the position shown in the figure, and suppose, moreover, that the current be flowing through the coils of the electromagnet in such a direction as to produce a south pole at A, and a north pole at B, and that the permanent magnet has its north pole at N, and its south pole at S. Then an attraction will take place between the poles of the permanent and the electromagnet, which will cause the latter to be moved around its axis in the direction of the arrow.

If the current continued to flow steadily through the coils of the electromagnet, the movement of the magnet would cease as

THE TRANSMISSION OF POWER.

soon as its poles came immediately over the poles of the permanent magnet. At this moment, by means of the commutator C, the current is reversed in the electromagnet by reversing its polarity. Under these conditions, aided by the momentum of the moving electromagnet, repulsion is produced between the poles N and A, and the rotation is continued in the same direction until the pole A, of the electromagnet comes over the pole S, of the permanent magnet, when the commutator again reverses the direction of the current. On this account the pull will not be uniform in such a machine at all positions of the electromagnet. Moreover, if the machine were to stop with its electromagnetic poles vertically over the permanent magnetic poles, it would require a mechanical motion before the current could again produce continued rotation.

The next important development, historically, was that made by Elias, who

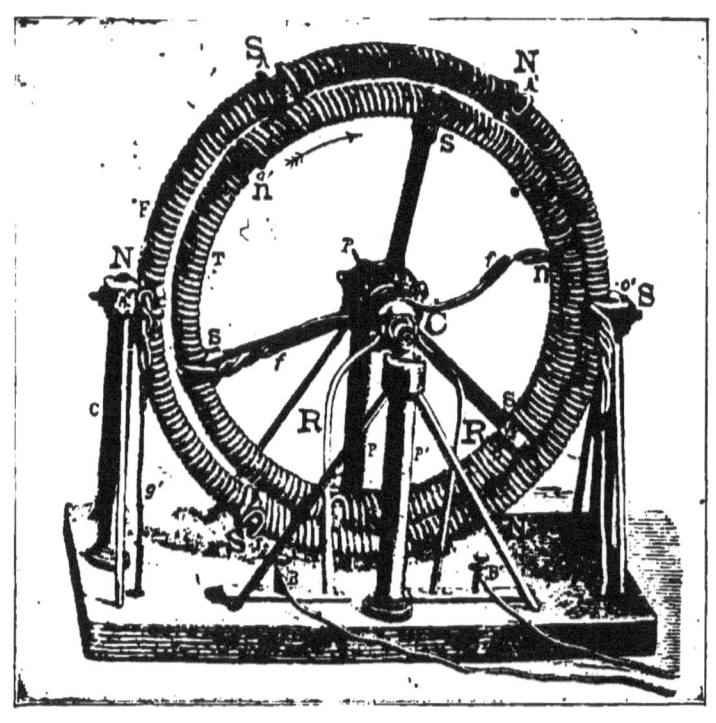

Fig. 18.—Elias' Motor.

in 1842 designed the motor shown in Fig. 18. Here, two coaxial iron rings are supported in the same vertical plane. The outer ring is fixed and the inner ring is movable about its axis. In this form of motor it will be noticed that, instead of employing a permanent magnet for the fixed magnet, an electromagnet is employed. This marks a considerable advance in the art; for, while it is now obvious that a fixed electromagnet is equivalent to a fixed permanent magnet, yet at the early date of which we are speaking, this was by no means an obvious matter. In fact, the earlier motors were constructed, as we have seen, with permanent magnets, while the modern motor, when of any considerable size, is invariably provided with electromagnets.

Broadly, then, an electromagnetic motor consists of two parts, in one of which the magnetic flux is fixed, and in the other the magnetic flux is movable, being changed at suitable intervals by the action of a commutator. The fixed part is called the *field magnet*, and the magnetically moving part the *armature*. In nearly all cases it is the magnetically moving part which rotates, the field magnets being usually fixed and the armature moving; but, as we have seen, this is not essential, since action and reaction are always equal and opposite, and we may have the magnetically fixed part rotary, and the magnetically moving part at rest. In order conveniently to distinguish between the mechanically moving and the magnetically moving parts, the name *stator* is sometimes applied to the part which is mechanically fixed, and the name *rotor* to the part which rotates, no matter what their magnetic condition may be.

Referring again to Fig. 18, the outer

fixed ring constitutes the field, and the inner movable ring the armature. Both field and armature are so wound with coils of insulated wire as to produce six poles at equal angular distances around their circumference, adjacent poles being of opposite polarity, as indicated by the letters *N, S, N, S, N, S,* in the field, and *n, s, n, s, n, s,* in the armature.

In this early form of motor, instead of employing the same current to excite both the field and armature, a separate current was employed to excite the field magnets, or, as it is now expressed, this was a *separately-excited motor*. The current passing through the armature was supplied through the terminals *B, B'*. The commutator *C*, which was so arranged that the brushes *R, R*, resting on the commutator segments, supplied current through the armature by the wires f, f, in a direction which produced the poles n, s, n, s, n, s, when the armature occupied the position indicated in the figure. Here the north poles in the armature attract the south poles of the field, and the south poles of the armature attract the north poles of the field, in such a manner as to cause the armature to be pulled around clockwise, or in the direction of the arrow. As soon as the poles in the armature come beneath the field poles, the armature poles are reversed by the brushes changing the segments upon which they rest at the commutator, and thus reversing the direction of current and the polarity of the armature, so that, aided by momentum, the armature poles repel the field poles nearest to them, and attract those ahead of them, thus maintaining a continuous rotation.

THE TRANSMISSION OF POWER. 113

This early type of machine must be regarded as exhibiting a considerable advance over its predecessors, and would, indeed, with comparatively small modification, make a motor approximating to the type of motors in modern use. It belongs to the type of machine now well established, called a *multipolar machine,* since it has more than two poles. It is, in fact, a *sextipolar,* or *six-pole machine.*

The type of machine shown in Fig. 10, was constructed by Froment in 1845. Here, as will be seen from an examination in the figure, a continuous rotatory motion is obtained by means of the action of electromagnets upon pieces of soft iron, called *armatures,* attached to the periphery of a movable wheel. The current is supplied from the battery B, to the motor through the terminals $T, T,$ and through the commutator C, to the magnets M, M, in such a manner that when the

FIG. 19.—FROMENT'S MOTOR.

circuit is completed, the magnets M, M, attract the soft iron bars A, A, A, and pull the armature around, say in a clockwise direction. As soon as the bars A, A, A, are opposite to the magnet poles, the current is cut off at the commutator, the armature continuing in rotation by its momentum until the bars are ready to be attracted by the next succeeding magnets, when the circuit is closed at the commutator. Successive magnetic impulses are thereby created, which result in a continuous rotatory motion of the armature. A number of motors, of different designs, but based on this general principle, were constructed by Froment.

Between 1845 and the present date, very many electromagnetic motors have been designed. With the limited space at our disposal we will not attempt any further to trace the early history of the electric motor, except to give a description of a very excellent form of early motor designed by Pacinotti in 1861, and represented in Fig. 20. Here the armature A, is mounted on a vertical axis between the poles of the electromagnets M_1, and M_2, which constitute the field magnets. The current is supplied through the terminals T'_1, and T'_2, say from T'_1 to the magnets M_1, and M_2, thence through the commutator apparatus C, to the armature, leaving by the terminal T'_2. The field magnets M_1, and M_2, are, therefore, excited in series with the armature, so that the machine is said to be *series-wound*.

The armature consists of an iron ring, wound at intervals with coils of insulated wire connected with the commutator, in such a manner as to produce poles in the armature between the polar projections N and S, of the field magnets. The armature turns so as to bring its poles directly opposite to the field poles. As it moves, however, the poles in the armature are

FIG. 20.—PACINOTTI'S MOTOR.

shifted by the action of the commutator, so that a continuous rotation takes place. Like all electromagnetic motors this machine, when independently driven as a dynamo, is capable of producing an E. M. F. provided the field magnets are suitably excited. The handle and disc shown behind the motor, were intended for the purpose of demonstrating this fact.

CHAPTER V.

ELEMENTARY THEORY OF THE MOTOR.

HAVING thus briefly traced some of the early history of electric motors, we will proceed to the theory of their operation.- Although this theory could readily be deduced from any of the motors we have considered, yet it will, perhaps, be preferable to base it upon a more modern type of motor, such as the machine shown in Fig. 21. This machine is of the *bipolar* type. It has two field poles N and S, produced by the magnetizing coils M, M. Between these poles the armature A, is free to revolve. The commutator C, and pulley P, are carried by the armature shaft.

The brushes *B, B,* rest upon the commutator, and supply the current to the armature from the main terminals *T, T,*

Fig. 21.—Bipolar Electric Motor.

in such a manner as to produce in it two poles, *n* and *s*, midway between the poles *N* and *S*, of the field magnet. The armature is, therefore, pulled around in the direction of the arrow, and, as it revolves, the current entering the armature is commuted in such a manner as to maintain the armature poles at their positions in the vertical plane.

The power of an electric motor depends upon two things; viz.,

(1) Upon the pull it exerts at the circumference of its pulley, and,

(2) Upon the speed at which it runs.

The greater the pull, and the greater the speed at which that pull is delivered, the greater the activity of the motor.

Since it is the *electro-dynamic force* which causes the rotation of a motor, it is clear that the pull, which will be exerted at the circumference of the pulley, will vary with the diameter of the pulley. It is customary to speak of the effect of this

122   THE ELECTRIC MOTOR AND

electro-dynamic force as the *torque*, a word derived from the Latin verb to twist. Suppose the electro-dynamic force of the motor

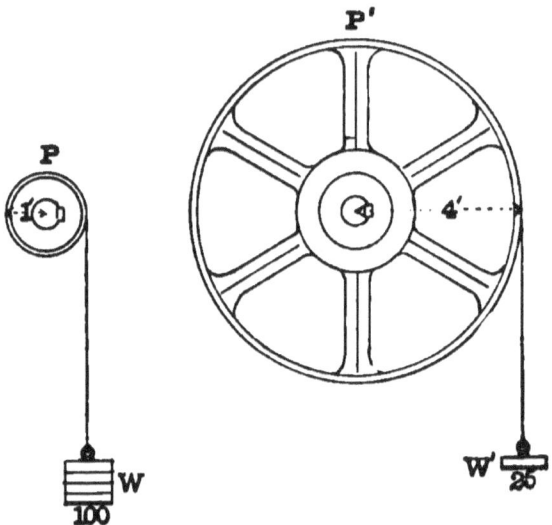

Fig. 22.—Torque Exerted upon Shafts by Weights Suspended over a Pulley.

were capable of exerting a twist or torque about the axis of the armature, represented by the pull of 100 pounds' weight, suspended over a pulley *P*, Fig. 22, 1 foot in radius; then it will be evident that if the pulley were exchanged for one 4 feet in radius, as shown at *P'*, in the same figure, the motor would only be capable of lifting a weight of 25 pounds sus-

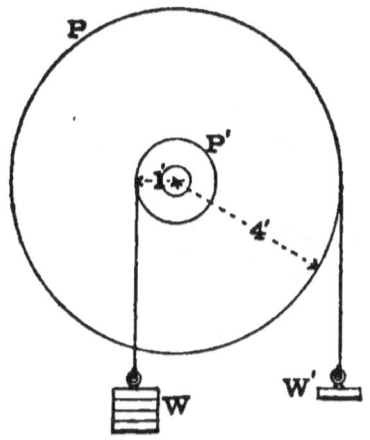

Fig. 23.—Equilibrium of Two Equal and Opposite Torques.

pended over this pulley; or, a torque of 100 pounds at a radius of one foot is the same as that exerted by 25 pounds at a radius of four feet. In fact it is clear that if the two pulleys *P* and *P'*, were mounted side by side on the same shaft, and the weights W and W', suspended from their peripheries on opposite sides, the torques exerted would be equal

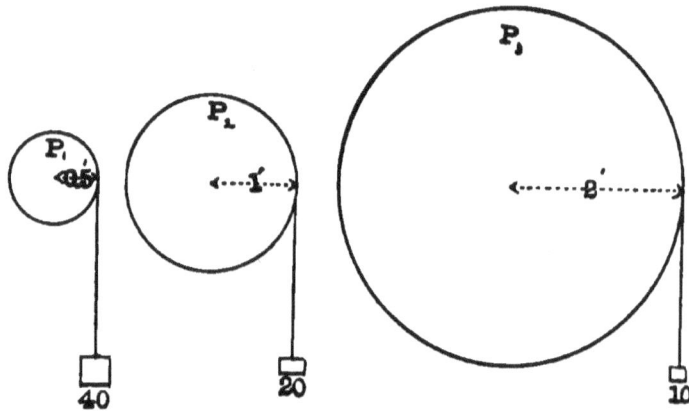

Fig. 24.—Diagrams of Torque.

and opposite, or the shaft would remain in equilibrium, as in Fig. 23.

Fig. 24, represents a torque of 20 pounds-feet, acting about the axis of each of the three pulleys P_1 P_2, and P_3; for, at P_1, we have a force of 40 pounds' weight acting at a radius of 1/2 a foot = 20 pounds-feet; at P_2, we have a force of 20 pounds' weight acting at a radius of 1 foot = 20 pounds-feet; and, at P_3, we have a force of 10 pounds' weight acting at a radius of 2 feet = 20 pounds-feet. It is evident, that the torque of a motor does not imply any particular size of the pulley on the motor; for, if a pulley of large diameter be employed, the force at its periphery will be comparatively small, while if a pulley of small diameter be employed, the force at its periphery will be comparatively great.

In the same way, the amount of work which a motor exerting a given torque will perform, during one complete revolution of its armature or pulley, does not imply any particular diameter of the pulley; but, if the pull to be exerted is given, then the limiting diameter, at which that pull can be exerted is known. Thus if a motor exerts a torque of 20 pounds-feet independently of the speed at which it runs, and the pulley P_1, of Fig. 24 be employed on its shaft, with a radius of half a foot, the motor will just be capable of lifting 40 pounds' weight on the periphery of the pulley; and, in one complete revolution, the pulley will raise this weight through a distance equal to its own circumference; namely, to $1/2 \times 6.2832 = 3.1416$ feet, and will, therefore, do an amount of work equal to $3.1416 \times 40 = 125.66$ foot-pounds $= 170.4$ joules. If, however, the pulley P_2, be employed, with a radius of one foot, the motor will just lift a weight of 20 pounds over its periphery; and, in one complete revolution, will do an amount of work equal to 6.2832 feet $\times 20$ pounds $= 125.66$ foot-pounds $= 170.4$ joules. Finally, if the pully P_3, be employed, the weight, which the motor will lift over its periphery, will be just 10 pounds, and its circumference being 2 × 6.2832 = 12.5664 feet, the amount of work done by the motor in one revolution will be 12.5664 × 10 = 125.66 foot-pounds = 170.4 joules; or, as we have already stated, the work done by a given torque in a given number of revolutions is independent of the radius of the pulley. If the pulley be large, the weight raised will be small, but the lift per revolution great, while, if the pulley be small, the weight raised will be great, but the lift per revolution small. On the other hand, if the weight to be lifted be known, the size of the pulley will be limited by the torque of the motor. Thus, a motor of 40 pounds-feet torque could not lift a weight of 5 pounds over a pulley more than 8 feet in radius.

The activity of a motor, being the work

done per second, will be equal to the product of the torque and 6.2832 times the number of revolutions per second. Thus, if

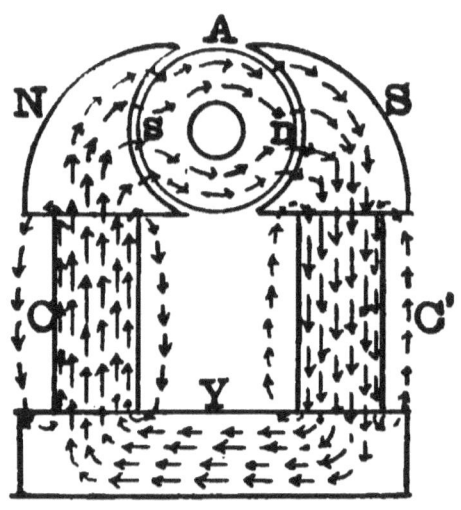

Fig. 25.—Magnetic Circuit of Motor Represented in Fig. 21.

a motor, exerting a steady torque of 50 pounds-feet, runs at 1,200 revolutions a minute, or 20 revolutions per second, the activity may be reckoned directly as 50 × 6.2832 × 20 = 6283.2 foot-pounds per second. A similar calculation will show that the activity of the motor would be the same with pulleys P_2 and P_3. For, although with the larger pulleys the peripheral speed in feet per second would be greater, yet the weights they would raise would be correspondingly smaller.

The torque exerted by a motor is the most convenient quantity for considering and discussing its mechanical power, and we will now proceed to consider how this torque varies with the electrical conditions in the motor.

To do this it will be necessary to consider the magnetic flux passing through the magnetic circuit of the motor. Fig. 25 represents diagrammatically the magnetic circuit of the motor shown in Fig. 21. Here the armature A, is situated between pole pieces N and S, and is separated from them by two annular air-gaps, one between the armature and N, and the other between the armature and S. The magnetic flux, which passes through this magnetic circuit, is produced by the magnetizing coils which are wound upon the iron cores, C, C'.

We have seen that the current strength produced by an electric source depends upon the E. M. F. of the source, and the resistance of its circuit. In the same way, in the magnetic circuit, the magnetic current, or magnetic flux, depends upon the magneto-motive force of the source, and upon the magnetic resistance of the circuit; or, just as we had,

$$\text{Electric current or flux} = \frac{\text{E. M. F.}}{\text{Electric Resistance}}$$

so here,

$$\text{Magnetic current or flux} = \frac{\text{M. M. F.}}{\text{Magnetic Resistance.}}$$

THE TRANSMISSION OF POWER. 131

Magnetic flux is estimated in *units of magnetic flux*, commonly called *webers*. A large motor may have a total magnetic flux of millions of webers, while a small motor, suitable for driving a table fan, may have a total flux in its circuit of only a few thousand webers.

The *unit of magneto-motive force*, usually written M. M. F., is commonly called the *gilbert*, and is the M. M. F. which would be produced by a current of 0.7958 amperes, flowing through one turn of wire. In other words, a current of one ampere, passing through one turn of wire; *i. e.*, one *ampere-turn*, produces an M. M. F. of 1.257 gilberts. The M. M. F. of a coil of wire is, therefore, proportional to the number of ampere-turns in it. If each of the coils on the magnets of Figs. 21 and 25, have 2,000 turns, and carries a steady current of 5 amperes, then the M. M. F. of the coils will be 5 × 2,000 = 10,000 ampere-turns = 12,570 gilberts in each coil, or 20,000 ampere-turns, and 25,140 gilberts in the complete circuit.

The amount of flux which will be produced by this M. M. F. will depend upon the magnetic resistance of the circuit; that is, on the magnetic resistance in the iron of the cores C C', the yoke Y, the pole-pieces N and S, the iron armature core A, and the air-gaps, on each side of the armature, through which the flux passes.

The magnetic resistance of a circuit, usually called its *reluctance*, is measured in *units of magnetic resistance* commonly called *oersteds*. The oersted is the resistance offered by a centimetre cube of air, that is to say, it is equal to the magnetic resistance which a column of air offers when it has a length of one centimetre and a cross-sectional area of one square centimetre. As in the case of an electric circuit, the electric resistance increases with the length of the circuit and decreases with the area of cross-section, so in the magnetic circuit, the magnetic resistance or reluctance increases with the length, and decreases with the area of cross-section. Thus, if each of the air-gaps in Fig. 25 is one centimetre long in the direction of the magnetic flux, and has an effective cross-sectional area, called *polar area*, of 1,000 square centimetres, then the reluctance of each air-gap will be $\frac{1}{1,000} = 0.001$ oersted, and the total reluctance in the air 0.002 oersted.

The reluctance of most substances is

practically the same as that of air, and is not affected by the quantity of flux which passes through it. In the case of iron, however, the magnetic reluctance is very small as compared with air, provided the magnetic flux through it is not very dense. When, however, the magnetic flux is very powerful, so that a great number of webers pass through each square inch of cross-sectional area, the iron is said to become *magnetically saturated*, and then offers a greatly increased reluctance. Thus, at a density of 5,000 webers-per-square-centimetre, which is commonly called a density of 5,000 *gausses*, the gauss being the *unit of magnetic density*, the reluctance of a cubic centimetre of iron is only about $\frac{1}{2,000}$th that of the reluctance of a cubic centimetre of air; but at a density of 16,000 webers-per-square-centimetre, or at 16,000 gausses;

THE TRANSMISSION OF POWER.   135

i. e., 16 *kilogausses*, the reluctance of a cubic centimetre of soft iron may be $\frac{1}{250}$th that of air. The *specific reluctance* of iron in terms of air; *i. e.*, its *reluctivity*, varies with the density of the flux passing through it, and also with the quality of the iron. The density of flux usually employed in motors containing cast iron in their magnetic circuit, is not more than 8,000 or 9,000 gausses; while in motors, employing soft wrought iron or soft steel, the density which may be employed is 12,000 to 15,000 gausses. There is, therefore, a considerable magnetic advantage in employing soft iron, or cast steel, in place of ordinary gray cast iron, in the magnetic circuits of dynamos and motors, since the former have a much lower magnetic resistance.

If, in Fig. 25, we assume that the total

reluctance of the iron of the magnetic circuit be 0.003 oersted, then the total reluctance in the circuit composed of iron and air, will be $0.003 + 0.002 = 0.005$ oersted, and the magnetic flux passing through the circuit will be

$$\frac{25,140 \text{ gilberts}}{0.005 \text{ oersteds}} = 5,028,000 \text{ webers.}$$

Fig. 25, shows that some of the magnetic flux does not pass through the armature, but through the air on each side of the field magnets. All such *stray flux* not passing through the armature is useless for the purpose of rotating the armature, and is, therefore, called *leakage flux*. *Magnetic leakage* necessarily occurs because there is no known magnetic insulator. An electric current can be restricted by the use of insulators to the conductors conveying it, such as air, dry wood, rubber, etc., but dry wood, rubber, glass and all known materials except the magnetic metals, conduct magnetic flux with equal facility; *i. e.*, have practically the same reluctivity. Consequently, some of the magnetic flux produced in the circuit by the M. M. F. of the field coils, will pass uselessly through the surrounding air. The useful magnetic flux is that which passes through the armature. The leakage can be reduced by diminishing the reluctance in the armature circuit relatively to the reluctance of the leakage paths surrounding the cores.

If the cross-section of the armature A, be known in square inches, the total useful flux passing through it may be readily estimated; for, it is usual to employ in the armature core a flux density of, approximately, ten kilogausses. This is a density well below saturation, and, since there are,

6.4516 square centimetres in a square inch, there will be, approximately, 64,500 webers of useful flux passing through each square inch of armature section, at right angles to the course of the magnetic flux through it. If, for example, the armature core be 39" long, and 20" in effective width, the cross-sectional area will be 780 square inches, and the probable amount of useful flux carried by the armature will be 780 × 64,500 = 5,030,000 webers.

The torque exerted by a motor armature depends upon three things; viz.,

(1) The useful flux passing through the armature in webers.

(2) The current strength passing through the armature in amperes.

(3) The number of turns of wire; *i. e.* the number of wires counted once around the surface of the armature.

If we multiply these three quantities together and divide by 85,155,000, we obtain the torque of the motor in pounds-feet.

If the motor shown in Fig. 21 has a current strength passing through its armature by the brushes B, B, of 20 amperes, a total number of wires counted once completely around the surface of the armature, amounting to 160, and a total flux passing through the field magnets amounting to 5,000,000 webers, then the torque exerted by the armature will be

$$\frac{20 \times 160 \times 5,000,000}{85,155,000} = 187.9 \text{ pounds-feet.}$$

If the pulley of this motor has a radius of one foot, then, neglecting frictions, the motor should be just able to start when a weight of 187.9 pounds is suspended from the periphery of its pulley.

It will be seen, from the foregoing, that the torque exerted by a motor depends upon the current strength passing through its armature. If we cut off the current from the armature, there will be no torque exerted by the motor, even though the field magnets be fully excited and their maximum magnetic flux produced. This must evidently be the case, since the cause of the electro-dynamic force is the mutual interaction of the field flux with the flux produced by the current through its armature wires, and the latter ceases on the cessation of the current.

We may now inquire into the causes which determine the speed of a motor. Let us suppose, for example, that the motor shown in Fig. 21, has its field magnets excited from some independent source, so that the amount of flux which passes

THE TRANSMISSION OF POWER. 141

through the armature may be regarded as constant, and equal to, say, 5,000,000 webers. If the armature be connected through its brushes, B, B, with a constant electric pressure, say, for example, with a pair of mains having a constant pressure of 10 volts, then the current strength, which will tend to pass through the armature, will be controlled by Ohm's law. Thus, if the resistance of the armature were $\frac{1}{10}$th of an ohm, the current strength, which would tend to pass through the armature at rest, would be 10 volts divided by $\frac{1}{10}$th ohm = 100 amperes. If the number of wires upon the surface of the armature be 100, counted once around, we have seen that the torque exerted by the armature, with this current strength, will be

$$\frac{100 \text{ amperes} \times 5{,}000{,}000 \text{ webers} \times 100 \text{ wires}}{85{,}155{,}000} = 587.3 \text{ pounds-feet.}$$

Supposing the belt to have been thrown off the pulley of the motor; then under this powerful torque the motor will be started in rapid rotation. As soon as the armature commences to revolve through the flux produced by the field magnets, it generates in the armature winding an E. M. F. which is counter or opposite to the current supplied to the armature. In other words, the revolving motor armature commences to act as a dynamo armature, opposing the current strength received from the mains. The effect of this C. E. M. F. is to reduce the amount of current received by the motor. If, for example, the armature revolves at such a rate as to generate a C. E. M. F. of 5 volts, the effective E. M. F. acting in its circuit will be $10 - 5 = 5$ volts, and the current will be reduced to 5 volts divided by $\frac{1}{10}$th of an ohm, or to 50 amperes. Similarly, if the speed at which the armature runs is sufficiently increased to develop a C. E. M. F. of 9 volts, the effective E. M. F. in this circuit will be $10 - 9 = 1$ volt, and the current will be reduced to 1 volt divided by $\frac{1}{10}$th ohm = 10 amperes. The armature, therefore, accelerates until such a speed is reached as will limit the current passing through it to just the value which is necessary in order to overcome the torque imposed on the motor; *i. e.*, the *resisting torque.*

The resisting torque will be very small if the motor be disconnected from its belt, being made up only of the frictions of bearings, brushes, etc.; while, if the belt be thrown on the motor, and it be connected with a heavy load, the resisting torque may be very considerable. The current strength required to overcome this torque is determined, as we have seen, by the flux through the motor, and by the number of turns of wire lying upon its armature. Consequently, the speed of an armature will automatically assume that value at which the *effective E. M. F.;* namely, the difference between the driving and C. E. M. F's., just enables this current strength to be supplied through the armature resistance.

A ten HP motor, separately excited, may be capable of developing an E. M. F. in its armature of 13 volts, for every revolution that it makes per second; that is to say, if the armature be set in rotation, in any manner, at the speed of one revolution per second, or 60 revolutions per minute, it will generate as a dynamo an E. M. F. of 13 volts. If its speed be altered to 3 revolutions per second, its E. M. F.

will be 39 volts. If now this motor, disconnected from its load, be connected with a pair of mains having a constant pressure between them of 208 volts, the armature will run at a speed of, approximately, 16 revolutions per second, or 960 revolutions per minute, and thereby generate an E. M. F. counter or opposed to the E. M. F. of the mains, equal to $16 \times 13 = 208$ volts; for, the resisting torque, made up of friction in the armature, will be very small, and if the speed of the motor falls below 16 revolutions per second, or 960 revolutions per minute, the current strength, which will pass through the armature, will be so rapidly increased that a powerful electro-dynamic torque will be exerted upon the armature causing it to accelerate, and so regain its full speed.

If there were no friction whatever in the

armature, which of course is impossible, there would, of course, be no current and no energy required to drive the armature, and if the pressure at its terminals from the mains were 208 volts, the motor would have to generate a C. E. M. F. of exactly 208 volts, so that by Ohm's law no current would pass through it and its speed would be steady at exactly 16 revolutions per second. If, however, a heavy load be thrown on the motor producing a powerful resisting torque of, say 100 pounds-feet, then the current strength, which will be necessary to pass through the armature in order to produce this torque, may be, say 20 amperes, and if the resistance of the armature be 1 ohm, the C. E. M. F. must drop to 188 volts in order that the driving E. M. F. shall permit 20 amperes to pass through this resistance; namely, $208 - 188 = 20 \div 1 = 20$

THE TRANSMISSION OF POWER.   147

amperes. The speed on the motor, when loaded will, therefore, drop to $\frac{188}{13} = 14.46$ revolutions per second, or 867.6 revolutions per minute.

Summing up, therefore, if a motor be separately excited, and be connected with a pair of *constant-potential mains;* i. e., a pair of mains maintained at an electrically constant difference of pressure or voltage, the speed at which it will run, will depend upon the number of wires lying upon its armature. If the armature have a large number of fine wires, its speed will be comparatively slow, since its dynamo action and C. E. M. F. for a given speed, will be great; or, in other words, the speed required to produce a given C. E. M. F. will be small. But if the number of wires on the armature be small, the speed at which it will have to run to develop a given C. E. M. F. will be great. As the torque imposed on the motor, or its load is increased, its speed will diminish in order to allow the necessary increase of current to pass through the motor to overcome this torque, and the amount of drop in speed will depend upon the resistance of the armature. If the resistance of the armature be comparatively great, the drop of pressure in the armature will be great, and the speed must fall off considerably; while, if the resistance of the armature be small, a comparatively small diminution in speed will, by Ohm's law, permit a comparatively large increase of current strength and torque.

Again, if the pressure on the mains with which an armature is connected be increased, the motor speed must increase in order to develop a correspondingly greater C. E. M. F. Thus, if a motor runs, light-loaded, at a speed of 500 revolutions per minute, when connected with a pair of 110-volt mains, it will run with the same excitation at, approximately, 1,000 revolutions per minute, when connected with a pair of 220-volt mains. This is evident, since, approximately, the same small current strength will have passed through it in each case, and the C. E. M. F. developed by the motor armature, must be nearly 110 volts in the first case, and nearly 220 volts in the second.

We have hitherto assumed that the amount of flux passing through the armature was constant, owing to separate excitation of the field magnets. It is evident, however, that if the flux passing through the armature be varied, the speed will also vary. Thus, if the machine already considered, which had a flux of 5,000,000 webers, and 100 wires on its armature, when connected with a pressure of 10 volts, made a speed of 10 revolutions per second, or 600 revolutions per minute; then, if we reduce the flux passing through the armature by one half, or to 2,500,000 webers, the speed will be practically doubled, or increased to 20 revolutions per second, or 1,200 revolutions per minute. This is for the reason that the armature must run faster through the weaker flux in order to generate a given C. E. M. F. If one revolution per second produced one volt in a stronger flux, two revolutions per second would be required, per volt, in the weaker flux. Consequently, we may always increase the speed of a motor by weakening its field flux; *i. e.*, by diminishing the current strength circulating in the field coils, and their M. M. F. There will, of course, be a limit to the degree at which this acceleration can be produced, since, if the flux is very much weakened, the flux produced by the current in the armature winding will overpower that of the field, and may actually reverse it, thus tending to destroy the C. E. M. F. of the armature, diminishing its torque indefinitely, and requiring an indefinitely high speed to check the current strength, and the machine will therefore stop. On the other hand, if we increase the current strength passing through the field magnet coils, and so increase their M. M. F., they will develop a greater magnetic current or flux in the magnetic circuit of the machine, including the armature, and this increased flux will produce the C. E. M. F. required from the motor at a correspondingly reduced speed.

In practice, motors are not usually separately excited, but are excited by a current obtained from the mains supplying the armature. The field winding may be connected either in series with the armature, producing what is called a *series-*

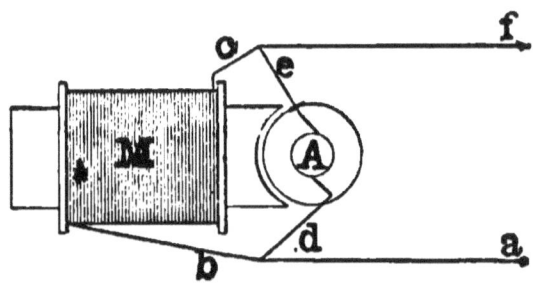

Fig. 26.—Diagram of Shunt Winding.

wound motor, or in shunt with the armature, producing what is called a *shunt-wound motor*. Fig. 26, represents diagrammatically the connections of a shunt-wound motor. Here the ends b and c, of the magnetic coils M, are connected in shunt with the ends d and e, of the armature A. a and f, are the constant-potential mains. If the resistance of the magnet M, be assumed constant, by Ohm's law the current strength through it must be constant, and the effect is the same as though the motor were separately excited. The strength of current, which the armature can carry continuously, depends upon its size, winding and construction. The drop of pressure, which its full-load current will produce, usually varies between 2 per cent. and 10 per cent. of the terminal pressure; that is to say, if the pressure between the mains a and f, be 500 volts, then the full-load drop in the armature will usually vary between 50 volts in a small motor, and 10 volts in a large motor, the C. E. M. F. at full load being respectively 450 and 490 volts. The drop in speed of such a motor will, therefore, usually vary between 10 per cent. and 2 per cent., according to the size of the machine, and, within these limits, the machine automatically regulates its speed according to the load.

The connections of a series-wound motor are shown in Fig. 27. Here the magnet

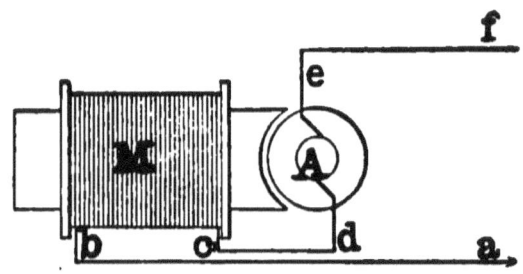

Fig. 27.—Diagram of Series Winding.

coil M, is in series with the armature A, between the mains a and f; that is to say the current from the mains passes successively through the magnet M, and armature A. When such a machine is on light load, with a small torque, the current strength passing through the machine will be comparatively small, and the M. M. F. of this current in the field coils will be small, producing thereby a small magnetic flux through the armature. The speed of the armature will, therefore, be comparatively great. If, however, the torque on the motor; *i. e.*, its load, be increased, the current passing through the motor will automatically increase, increasing thereby the M. M. F. and flux through the armature, thus reducing the speed. On this account, as well as owing to the drop of pressure in the resistance of the armature, a series-wound motor is much more variable in its speed than is a shunt-wound motor, but a series-wound motor, especially in small sizes, is simpler to construct; for, its field-winding consists of but comparatively few turns of coarse wire, while a shunt motor field-winding consists of many turns of fine wire, in order to reduce as far as possible the current strength employed in magnetizing them.

A compound-wound motor is a motor whose field magnets are partly series-

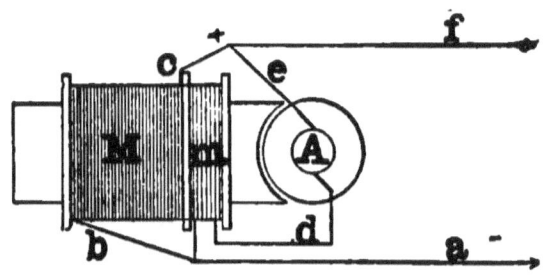

Fig. 28.—Diagram of Compound Winding.

wound and partly shunt-wound. Such a winding is diagrammatically represented in Fig. 28. Here the armature A, is in series with the coarse wire coils m, and these two are connected in shunt with the fine wire coil M. When no current passes through the armature, the field magnet M, is excited, while the series coil m, is unmagnetized. When the full-load current passes through the armature, the excitation of the series coil m, reaches its maximum. The M. M. F. of m, is counter or opposed to the M. M. F. of M, so that the magnetic flux is slightly weakened at full load, thereby necessitating a slight acceleration of the armature in order to develop its C. E. M. F. This acceleration may be adjusted so as to almost completely counterbalance the drop in speed, which would otherwise take place by virtue of the drop of pressure in the resistance of the armature, considered as a separately-excited machine. A compound-wound motor may, therefore, be adjusted so as to have a practically constant speed under all loads.

The activity absorbed by a motor is usually measured as the product of the terminal pressure in volts and the current strength in amperes. Thus, if the motor be connected with a pair of 220-volt mains, and be observed to take a total current of 10 amperes, then the activity absorbed by the motor will be 220 volts × 10 amperes = 2,200 watts = 1,622 foot-pounds-per-second = 2.2 kilowatts = 2.949 horse-power. If the motor were a perfect machine, expending no internal activity, under these conditions, it would do mechanical work at a rate of 2,200 watts, or 1,622 foot-pounds-per-second, but its actual efficiency would, probably, be about 82 per cent. in this size of machine, and the mechanical activity it would exert, would be $2{,}200 \times \frac{82}{100} = 1{,}804$ watts = 1,330 foot-pounds-per-second. The motor could, therefore, lift 1 pound 1,330 feet per second, or 133 pounds 10 feet per second, at this load.

THE TRANSMISSION OF POWER. 159

The efficiency of motors varies with their size. A very small motor, such as that employed for driving a desk fan, has an efficiency of, probably, only 30 per cent., while a 1 horse-power motor will, probably, have an efficiency of 60 per cent., and a 100 horse-power motor an efficiency of, probably, 90 per cent. The efficiency may be even still greater in larger sizes, although, of course, it can never reach 100 per cent., since some activity is sure to be lost within the motor.

It should be clearly borne in mind that all improvements, which have yet to be made in electro-dynamic motors, must be almost entirely confined to the directions of reduced speed or reduced cost, because the efficiency is already so comparatively high. If a 100 horse-power motor only wastes about 10 horse-power at full load, in its mechanical and electrical frictions, the best possible motor of this size could only save 10 horse-power under the same conditions. The direction, in which we may look forward to improvements in motors, lies, therefore, almost wholly in reducing their cost of construction and the speed at which they run.

The work absorbed by an electric motor from the circuit supplying it is conveniently measured in units called *kilowatt-hours*, a kilowatt-hour being an amount of work equal to that performed by an activity of one kilowatt maintained steadily for one hour. A kilowatt-hour is equal to 1.34 (roughly 1 1/3) horse-power-hours, or to 3,600,000 joules, or 2,663,000 foot-pounds. In Great Britain the kilowatt-hour is called the "Board of Trade Unit."

The work consumed by an electric motor is usually measured by a meter placed in its circuit. The meter may be a wattmeter, in which case its dial will show the total amount of work received by the motor in kilowatt-hours; or it may be an ampere-hour meter, whose indications, multiplied by the pressure of the circuit, assumed as uniform, will give the total amount of work consumed. Thus, if a motor connected with a 220-volt, constant-potential circuit, is shown to have received 5,000 ampere-hours in a month, by the record of an ampere-hour meter, the total work it has received will be $5,000 \times 220 = 1,100,000$ watt-hours $= 1,100$ kilowatt-hours.

CHAPTER VI.

STRUCTURE AND CLASSIFICATION OF MOTORS.

TURNING now to the practical construction of motors, let us look at the motor shown in Fig. 29, and in order to understand its construction, let us take it apart and study it in detail as shown in Fig. 30. In these figures, corresponding numerals represent corresponding parts. 1, is the completed armature, mounted on its shaft, with a commutator at one end, and with the insulated winding wrapped round and round the iron *core* or *body*, and suitably connected with the commutator. The shaft rests in journals 15 and 18, supported on pedestals 13 and 16. These bearings are *self-oiling;* that is to say, they contain oil which is continually poured upon the surface of the revolving shaft by

FIG. 29.—FORM OF ELECTRIC MOTOR.

the action of the rings 19, as will be later explained.

On the end of the shaft opposite to the commutator is secured the pulley 5. The pedestals themselves rest upon the cast-iron base plate 8, to which they are firmly secured by bolts. This base plate forms part of the magnetic circuit of the machine. Upon its smooth surface are bolted the field cores, 3, 3, on the heads of which stand the pole pieces 2, 2. The pole pieces are set in place after the magnets coils 4, 4, are set in position. The rocker arm 21, carries the two brush holders 22, 22, in insulated sockets at each extremity, and the brush holders, in their turn, clamp the metallic brushes 23, 23, which rest upon the surface of the commutator at diametrically opposite points. By moving the handle of the rocker arm, the diameter upon which the brushes bear on the commutator, called the *diameter of commutation*, can be varied within suitable limits; 24, are the cables connecting the brushes with the terminals 6 and 7, mounted

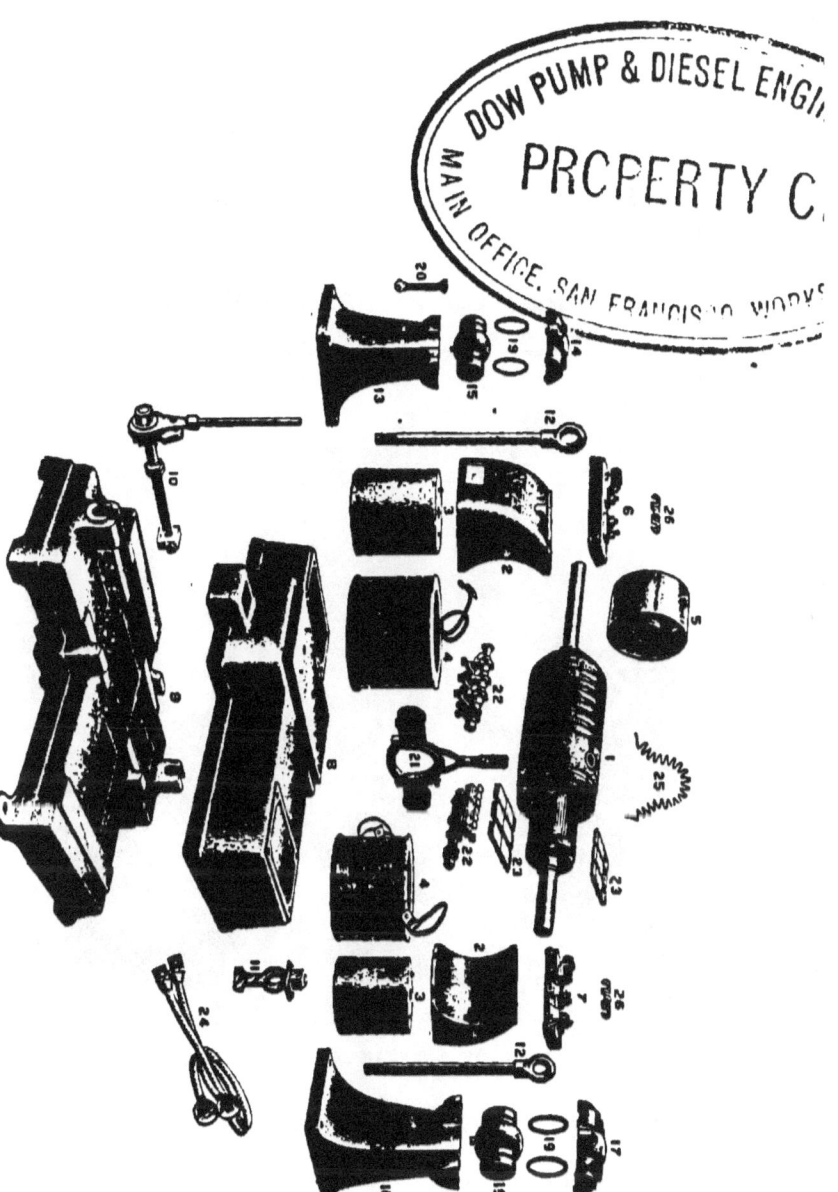

Fig. 30.—Details of Motor Shown in Fig. 29.

on a board above the pole-pieces, and to which the main leading wires are attached. The rods 12, 12, securely bolt the cores

FIG. 31.—FORM OF CONTINUOUS-CURRENT MOTOR.

and pole-pieces to the base plate, and also leave eye-bolts by which the machine can be readily slung.

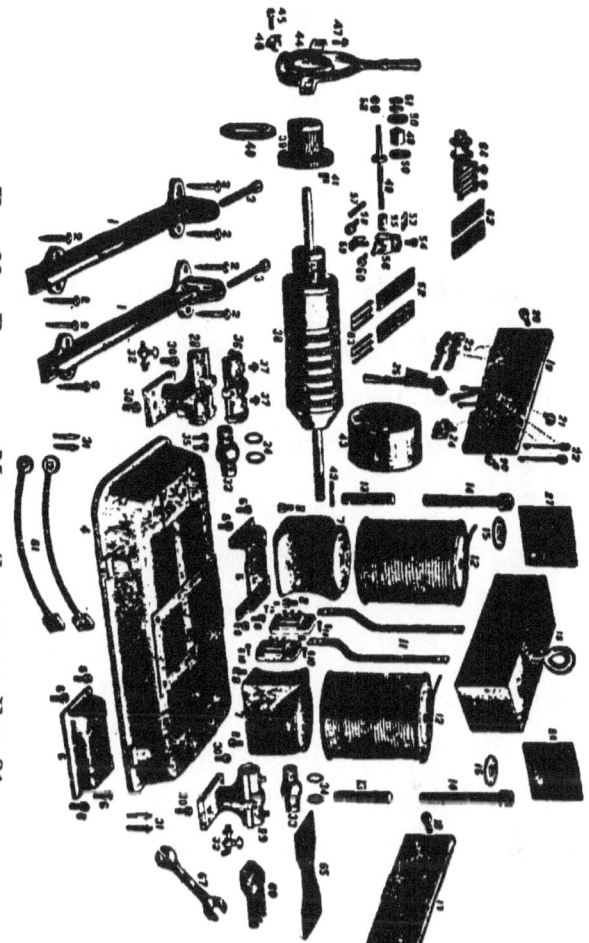

FIG. 32.—PARTS OF MOTOR SHOWN IN FIG. 31.

The motor shown in Fig. 31, differs from that in Fig. 29, in the fact that the armature and pole-pieces are supported close to the base, so that the field magnets are inverted. In other respects, however, the parts are similar in each motor. This motor is shown dissected in Fig. 32, where, as before, corresponding parts are marked with corresponding numerals. It is important to notice that in order to prevent the magnetic flux produced by the M. M. F. of the coils 12, from passing entirely through the cast iron base, the pole-pieces are supported on slabs of zinc 5, which introduces a greater reluctance into this path and enables almost all of the magnetic flux to pass through the armature core.

In order to obtain a better conception of the construction, we may now consider

THE TRANSMISSION OF POWER. 169

Fig. 33.—Motor with Ring Armature.

the separate parts of the motor in further detail, beginning with the armature. Broadly speaking, armatures may be divided into three classes; namely,

(1) Drum armatures.
(2) Ring armatures.
(3) Disc armatures.

Figs. 22, 29, 30, 31, and 32 represent *drum armatures;* that is to say, armatures which are simply drum-shaped or cylindrical in their appearance.

Fig. 34.—Motor with Gramme Ring Armature.

Fig. 33, represents a motor furnished with a *ring armature A A A.* Here the field magnets are placed inside the armature, as is sometimes the case, though more frequently the armature is placed inside the field, as is shown in Fig. 34,

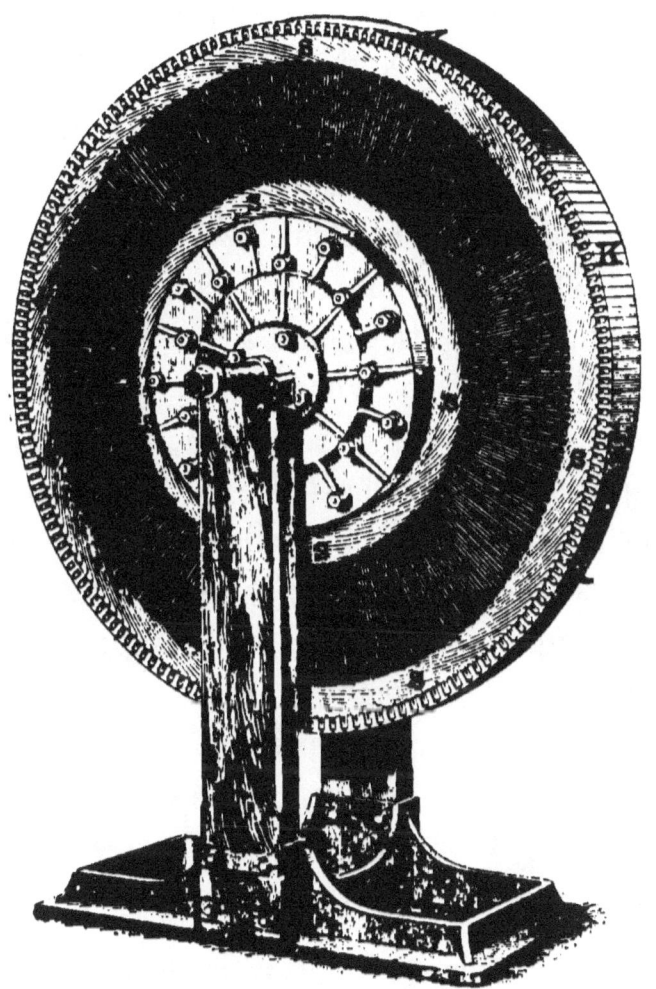

Fig. 35.—Disc Armature.

where the armature A, is placed between the poles N and S, of the magnet M.

An example of a *disc armature* is shown in Fig. 35. Here a number of insulated radial conductors C, C, are held like spokes in a wheel, and are connected together by conducting strips s, s, s, at the centre and edge of the wheel. In this armature the conducting bars k, k, k, on the periphery of the wheel, form the commutator upon which the collecting brushes are intended to rest. Fig. 36 represents the complete machine employing this armature. The magnets are here enclosed in a field frame, and present their polar surfaces to each other across the disc armature. Disc armatures are very seldom used in the United States.

A drum or ring armature consists essentially of three parts; namely,

Fig. 36.—Disc Armature Motor.

(1) The *core* or body, which is always of soft iron.

(2) The *exciting coils* of insulated copper wire, which are wound upon the core, and in which the E. M. F. is generated by revolution through the flux.

(3) The *commutator*, by means of

which the E. M. F.'s induced in the coils are united and co-directed so as to produce a continuous E. M. F. in the circuit; or, regarded from a different standpoint, the commutator distributes the current received from the external circuit through the armature winding, in such a manner as to produce a continuously acting torque.

Armature cores may be divided, from another standpoint into two classes; viz., the *smooth-core* and the *toothed-core*. Smooth-core armatures present a continuously smooth, cylindrical surface before the wire is wound upon them. Such a core is shown in Fig. 37. Here S, S, is a steel shaft, which carries two phosphor-bronze spiders, one of which only is seen at B. These spiders are clamped to the shaft and support between them the hollow core

C, C, which consists of a number of thin, soft iron plates, or annular discs, which after being assembled, are pressed together

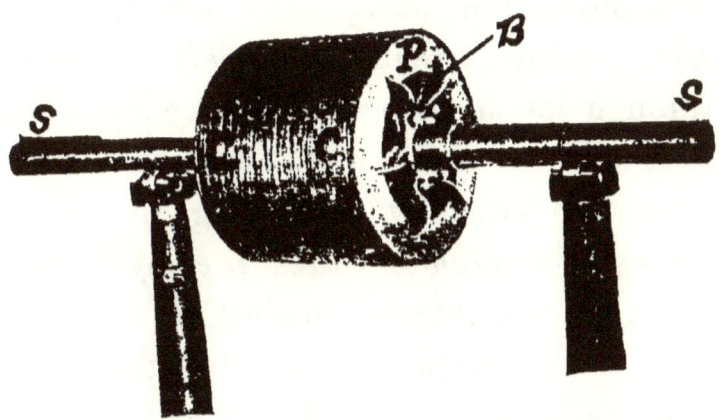

Fig. 37.—Smooth-Core Armature Body.

and then clamped by a spider between the end plates *P*.

In the early history of the art, armature cores were constructed of solid masses of soft iron; but it was soon found that such cores became intensely heated when revolved through the field flux, even though no insulated wire was wound upon their surfaces. This heating was owing to the fact that E. M. F.'s were induced in the conducting iron mass, which set up powerful electric currents, called *eddy currents*, through its substance. These eddy currents did no useful work, and expended power prejudicially in heating the core. By using *laminated cores;* i. e., by dividing the core into a number of separate discs, with their planes at right angles to its axis, while the passage of the magnetic flux is not impeded, since it passes directly through each disc, in its own plane, the eddy currents, which tend to develop in a direction at right angles to the plane of the discs, are very greatly checked and impeded on account of the resistance offered to their passage through the pile of discs. Consequently, the loss of power from eddy currents is very greatly reduced by this expedient of laminating the core, or building it of separate discs, and the process is invariably adopted except in the very smallest motors.

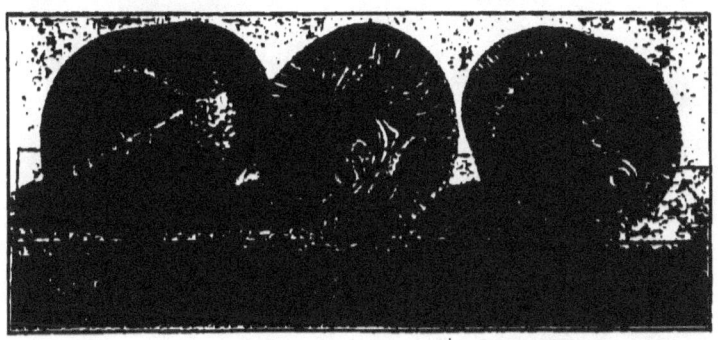

Fig. 38.—Toothed-Core Armature in Various Stages of Construction.

Toothed-core armatures are those which possess corrugated surfaces, like a cog wheel. Such a toothed-core armature is shown in Fig. 38 at *A*. It will be observed that the surface of this core is indented with grooves, running parallel to the axis of the shaft. In these grooves the conducting wires, protected by suitable insulating material, are subsequently laid. At *B*, the armature is shown with

FIG. 39.—ASSEMBLAGE OF LAMINATED ARMATURE CORE DISCS.

its winding in place, following the grooves. At *C*, the complete and covered armature is shown. Fig. 39, shows a method of assembling toothed-core armatures upon a shaft, so as to form, when completed, a drum armature. Here S, S, is the shaft, C, the assembled discs, and c, c, the discs ready to be assembled.

It will be observed that when completed, and wound with wire, both the toothed-core and the smooth-core armatures are alike, in that they both present

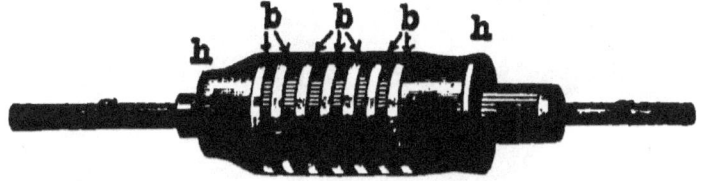

Fig. 40.—Completed Smooth-Core Armature.

a continuous cylindrical surface, but in the smooth-core armature this surface is formed entirely of insulated wire which completely covers and hides the iron core. In the toothed-core armature, however, the iron teeth or projections extend to the surface, and remain uncovered by wire, which only fills the grooves between adjacent teeth. Thus Fig. 40, shows a completed smooth-core, drum-armature, with the insulated conducting wire lying over its surface, parallel to the axis. In this armature it is necessary to hold the wire securely in place by binding the brass

FIG. 41.—COMPLETED TOOTHED-CORE ARMATURE.

wire b, b, b, tightly over mica strips and soldering it in position. The ends of the armature are covered by canvas supported on circular heads h, h.

Fig. 41, shows a completed toothed-core drum armature. Here, as will be seen, the external surface of the armature consists of iron, between the bands *b, b*.

Fig. 42 represents a portion of one of the discs of a toothed-core armature. The

Fig. 42.—Portion of Disc of Laminated Toothed-Core Armature.

circular holes are for the clamping bolts, while the grooves are intended for the reception of the insulated wires.

It will thus be seen that a toothed-core armature is much more solid and secure, when completed, than the smooth-core armature, and, partly for this reason, the toothed-core armatures have come into general use. It is evident that the toothed-core armature does not require bands on its surface to keep the wires in place. Moreover, the length of the air-gap or *entrefer;* that is to say, the distance between the iron in the armature and the polar faces of the field magnets, is greatly reduced, thereby reducing the reluctance of the magnetic circuit, and requiring much less M. M. F. in the field magnet coils to produce a given amount of flux through the armature.

Fig. 43 represents the winding of a toothed-core armature B. Here, as will be seen, the cotton covered wires are passed through the grooves. A, shows a complete armature with the wire connected to the commutator C.

Fig. 43.—Winding of Toothed-Core Armature.

A simple form of commutator, called a *two-part commutator* is shown in Fig. 44. Such a commutator would be suitable for commuting the current produced in a single loop of wire on an armature rotated in a

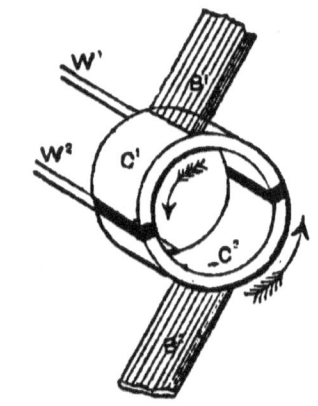

Fig. 44.—Diagram of Two-Part Commutator.

bipolar field. In this commutator the wire W^2, is connected to the segment C^2, and the wire W^1, to the segment C^1. Under these conditions, if the E. M. F. generated in the loop whose terminals are W^1 and W^2, be in such a direction that W^1, is positive and W^2, negative, the current will flow from W^1, to C^1, and out from the brush B^1, through the external circuit connecting the brushes, and return through the brush B^2, the segment C^2, and the wire W^2. After a quarter of a revolution has been effected from the position shown, and in the direction indicated by the arrows, the brush B^1, will rest on the segment C^2, and the brush B^2, on the segment C^1. At the same moment, however, if the commutator is properly placed, the E. M. F. which is being generated in the loop will be reversed by its passage before the magnet poles. W^2, will therefore be the positive pole under the new conditions. The current will consequently flow from W^2, to C^2, and brush B^1, and return after traversing the external circuit through B^2, segment C^1, and wire W^1. Consequently, although the E. M. F. in the armature has been reversed, the brush B^1, is still positive, and the current in the external circuit preserves its direction. No matter how many bars a commutator may possess, and no matter how many wires or loops are undergoing commuta-

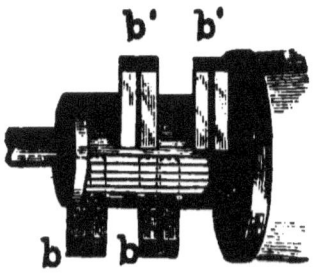

FIG. 45—ARRANGEMENT OF BRUSHES ON A COMMUTATOR.

tion, the effect will be essentially the same as that here described.

The arrangement of brushes resting in contact with a commutator, for such a motor as is shown in Fig. 31, is represented in Fig. 45. Here b, b, b^1, b^1, are two pairs of brushes, each pair being connected electrically together and resting upon the commutator bars. The brushes consist of metallic strips or bundles of wire, usually of copper, but sometimes consisting of carbon blocks. They are held in place by devices called *brush-holders*, a form of which is shown in Fig. 46. Springs placed in these brush-

FIG. 46.—BRUSH-HOLDERS.

holders maintain a uniform electric pressure between the brush and the commutator. After the brushes have been so set as to press upon opposite segments of the commutator, they can be rotated together into any suitable position by the *rocker arm*, which is represented at 21, in Fig. 30, and at 44, in Fig. 32.

We have seen that in all motors a certain amount of energy is uselessly expended in the friction between the revolving shaft and its supports. In order to lessen this as much as possible the bearings are kept well lubricated. In practice this is almost invariably secured by means of *automatic oilers*, that is, by bearings which automatically keep the rubbing surfaces lubricated. Such an automatic, self-oiling bearing is shown in Fig. 47. Here the shaft is supported in the sleeve S, of a special alloy, called *Babbitt metal*, having grooves cut in its interior, so as to distribute the oil freely over the revolving surface of the shaft by the action of rotation. This action is facilitated by the action of two rings R, R, which rest upon the shaft in grooves cut into the Babbitt metal sleeve. These rings dip beneath the surface of the oil in the

FIG. 47.—AUTOMATIC SELF-OILING BEARING.

reservoir O. As the shaft revolves it sets the ring into rotation, although the rotation may be many times less rapid than that of the shaft. The rings carry oil on their surfaces up into the grooves and distribute this over the shaft. The oil, after passing through the bearing, drips again into the reservoir O. The level of the oil in the reservoir can be observed by means of the gauge glass G. The sleeve S, and

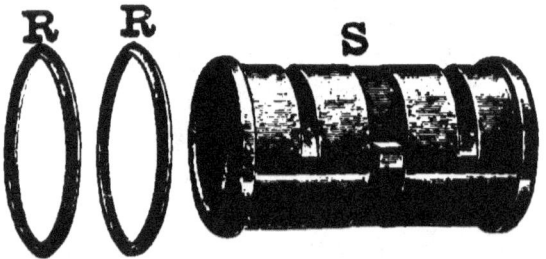

FIG. 48.—DETAILS OF SELF-OILING BEARING.

its brass rings, are shown in greater detail in Fig. 48.

The field magnets, the function of which is to produce the flux passing through the armature, consist essentially of coils of insulated wire, provided with cores and pole

THE TRANSMISSION OF POWER. 191

pieces, shaped so as to produce an annular or cylindrical space for the rotation of the armature. In Fig. 30, the field magnet cores, with their pole pieces, are shown

FIG. 49.—SKELETON OF MOTOR PARTS.

at 3 and 2, respectively. The coils of insulated wire which surround them are in practice wound on spools so that the entire coil can be readily removed from the core. Such a coil is shown at 4, in Fig. 30. The cast-iron base of the machine forms part of the magnetic circuit, as already mentioned.

Fig. 50.—Complete Motor of Type Shown in Fig. 49.

In Fig. 49, a skeleton representation of the different parts of a particular form of motor, is shown in place. Here the armature, with its commutator and pulley, is mounted between the pole pieces of the electromagnet as shown. In this machine, the field cores C, C, are clamped by bolts in recesses prepared for their reception in the cast-iron bed plate. A complete machine of the same type is shown in perspective in Fig. 50.

Since the torque of a motor depends upon the amount of flux passing through the armature, upon the current strength it carries, and upon the number of wires lying on the surface of the armature, it is evident that a powerful torque necessitates a powerful flux, a powerful current, and a great number of wires. As we increase these, we must increase the size of the machine. Consequently, powerful motors, are necessarily large, heavy motors.

It may be interesting to note the weight and dimensions generally given to motors of various sizes. A half-horse-power motor of good type, weighs about 100 pounds, or about 200 pounds per horse-power, and occupies a floor space of 18" × 10." A 5-horse-power motor, of good type, weighs about 600 pounds, or 120 pounds per horse-power, and occupies a floor space of 28" × 20". A 15-horse-power motor of good type, weighs about 1,500 pounds, or 100 pounds per horse-power, and occupies a floor space of 4' 6" × 3'. A 60-horse-power motor weighs about 6,000 pounds, or about 100 pounds per horse-power, and occupies a floor space of about 7' × 5', while a 250-horse-power motor would have a weight of about 25,000 pounds, or 100 pounds per horse-power, and a floor space of 11' × 6'. It will be seen, therefore, that small motors weigh about 200 pounds per horse-power—or 746 watts (roughly 750 watts)—of full-load mechanical output, and large motors about 100 pounds per horse-power. The slower

THE TRANSMISSION OF POWER. 195

the speed at which a motor is designed to run, the greater will be its weight, other things being equal.

It is convenient to remember that for motors up to 10-horse-power, the number of horse-power delivered is roughly equal to the number of kilowatts absorbed at the motor terminals. For example, a 6-horse-power motor, delivering, therefore, 4,476 watts mechanically, absorbs roughly 6 kilowatts, or 6,000 watts, at its terminals, whether the machine be built for circuits of 100 volts, 200 volts or 500 volts. This rule presupposes a commercial efficiency of 74.6 per cent. In large sizes the efficiency increases and the rule cannot, therefore, be relied upon. Thus a machine which has a full-load output of 120 horse-power, or about 90 KW, has an intake of, approximately, 100 KW.

The speed of motors depends upon their size and construction. If two motors have the same weight, floor space, efficiency, and cost, the one which has the slower speed of revolution is the better machine of the two, because, by rewinding it for the higher speed it could be made to have a greater output, that is to be the equivalent of a heavier machine. The speed of a 1/2-horse-power motor of good type is about 1,300 revolutions per minute at full-load; that of a 1-horse-power motor, about 1,000 revolutions per minute; of a 5-horse-power motor, 900 revolutions per minute; a 15-horse-power motor, 750 revolutions; a 120-horse-power motor, about 550 revolutions and a 250-horse-power motor, about 425 revolutions per minute.

Small motors are usually constructed with two field magnet poles, or belong to

THE TRANSMISSION OF POWER. 107

the bipolar type. Beyond a certain size, however, say 20-horse-power, it is usually more convenient and economical to con-

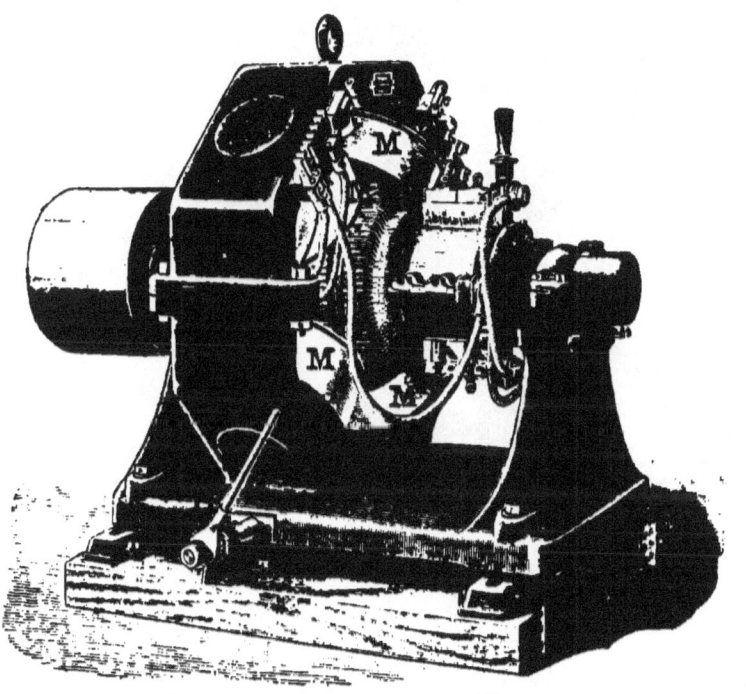

FIG. 51.—QUADRIPOLAR MOTOR.

struct motors with four or more poles, quadripolar motors being common between 20-HP and 500-HP.

A form of quadripolar motor is shown in Fig. 51. Here there are four magnets, *M, M, M, M*, and, consequently, four mag-

FIG. 52.—QUADRIPOLAR MOTOR.

netic circuits through the armature. There are also four sets of brushes, instead of two, as in bipolar machines, but opposite sets of brushes are connected together electrically, thus making a single pair of main terminals.

Another type of quadripolar motor is shown in Fig. 52. Here only two sets of brushes are employed, the winding and connection of the armature coils being such as to permit the use of two, instead of four brushes.

CHAPTER VII.

INSTALLATION AND OPERATION OF MOTORS.

THE installation of a small motor does not require any particular preparation. It is only necessary to bolt the base frame of the motor to the floor, and set the machine upon it. With heavy motors, however, suitable foundations are necessary in order to support them securely. In most cases a *belt tightener* is employed, whereby the tension of the belt can be adjusted by sliding the motor along its bed plate. This is represented in Figs. 51 and 52, where the handle *H*, enables this adjustment to be made readily. Belts should not be tightened so far as to add considerably to the friction of the shaft in its bearings, nor be left so loose as to slip or flap.

Where steady driving under all variations of load is a matter of importance, the shunt-wound motor; or, in some cases, the compound-wound motor, is employed, and, in fact, series-wound stationary motors are usually only employed in small sizes such as in fan motors.

By reference to the connections of the shunt-wound motor shown in Fig. 26, it will be seen that the armature is connected directly across the mains. If we assume that this connection is made with the armature at rest, and after the field circuit has been closed, so as to excite the field and produce the magnetic flux through the armature; then, since the resistance of the armature is necessarily small, a very powerful current will tend to flow through the armature, owing to the absence of any C. E. M. F. due to rota-

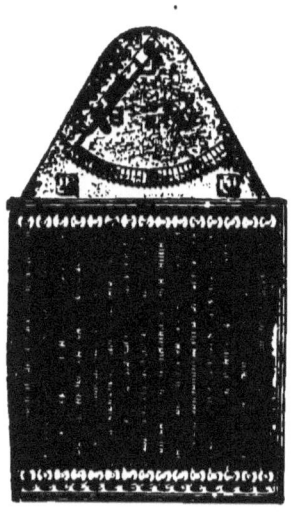

Fig. 53.—Starting Rheostat.

tion. This first inrush of current and violent resulting torque, are apt to be injurious to the motor. When, therefore, a shunt-wound motor is started from rest, it is necessary to insert a resistance in the armature circuit, so as to limit the amount of current which shall pass through the armature until it has been brought up to speed and enabled to produce a suffi-

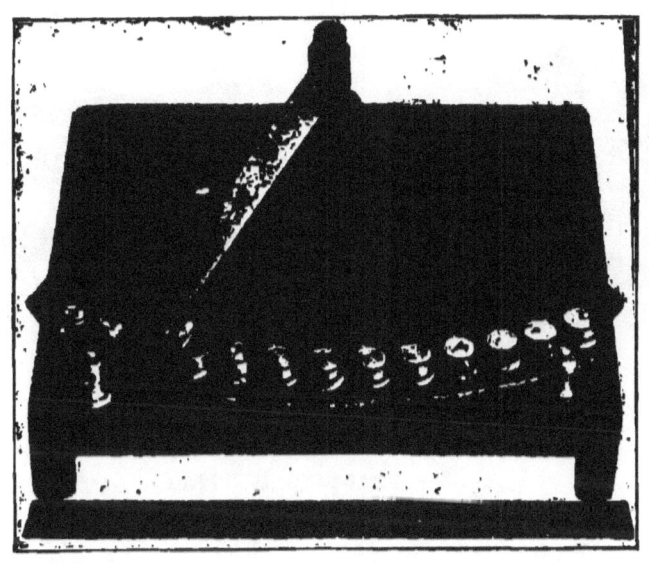

Fig. 54.—Starting Rheostat.

ciently powerful C. E. M. F. Such adjustable resistances are called *starting rheostats*. They consist essentially of coils of wire, usually of iron, mounted in a suitable frame, and connected with contact strips in such a manner as to permit their ready insertion or removal from the circuit by the movement of a handle.

Fig. 55.—Starting Rheostat.

A form of starting rheostat is shown in Fig. 53. Here coils of iron wire are mounted on a suitable frame and connected in series. By turning the switch S, over the contact points, a greater or smaller number of these coils may be

Fig. 56.—Installation of Shunt-Wound Motor.

included in the circuit. When the switch is on the extreme left contact point, no coils are in circuit, and when on the extreme right, all are in circuit. Fig. 54 shows a different type of starting rheostat intended for use with small motors. Here the resistance wire is imbedded in a suitable enamel on the lower surface of the cast-iron plate shown, and the switch serves, as before, to include more or less of this wire between the terminals. Fig. 55, shows a similar apparatus of larger sizes intended for use with more powerful motors.

Fig. 56 shows, in perspective, the ordinary method of installing a shunt-wound motor, and Fig. 57, the diagrammatic connections of the same. Similar letters refer to similar parts in both figures. It will be observed that a pair of mains MM, and

$M'\,M'$, being connected with a constant pressure of, say 110, 220, or 500 volts, according to the circuit, and the winding

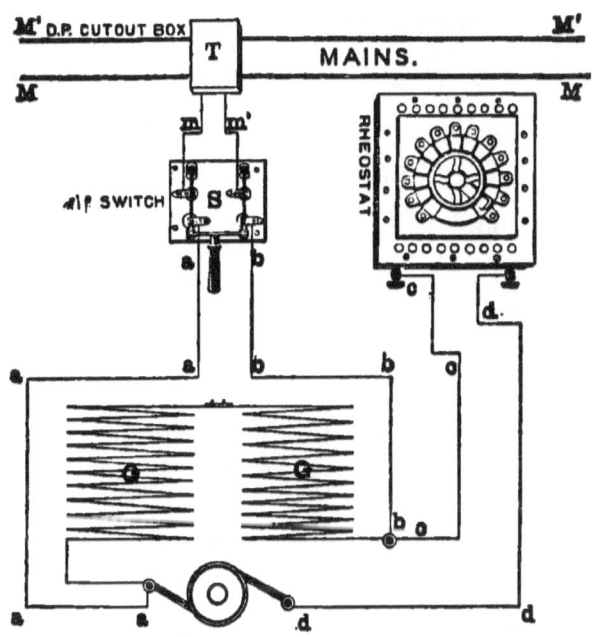

FIG. 57.—CONNECTIONS OF SHUNT-WOUND MOTOR.

of the motor, are connected with the motor through the switch S, and the cut-out box T. The switch S, consists of a handle attached to a pair of copper knife blades, in such a manner, that on depressing the handle, electrical connection is secured between the branch mains m, m', and the wires a and b, leading to the motor, while if the handle be raised, connection is instantly broken. The switch is called a *double-pole switch*, because it breaks contact both on the positive and negative sides of the circuit; *i. e.*, on one side, at each knife edge. The *cut-out box* T, contains a pair of *safety fuses* of lead wires, having such an area of cross section and resistance, that they will melt if the motor should receive an abnormal amount of current.

In order to start the motor from rest, it is usual to throw off the load in the driving machinery, as far as possible, so as to reduce the resisting torque on the motor as far as may be convenient. The handle H, of the rheostat R, is then so turned as to cut off the current or disconnect its circuit entirely. Under these circumstances, when the switch S, is thrown, so as to complete connection between the wires a and m, on one side, say the positive side, and b and m', on the negative side, then a comparatively feeble current will pass through the field-magnet coils G, G, and steadily excite them, this current being determined by the resistance of the coils and the pressure of the circuit. If now the handle H, be turned slowly so as to close the armature circuit through all the resistance in the rheostat, a current will pass through the wires b, c, the rheostat d, and armature a, and this current will start the motor from rest, provided the resisting torque is not too great.

As the armature accelerates, the resistance in the rheostat is cut out, and, when the motor reaches full speed, the handle is turned so as to cut out all the resistance. In order to stop the motor, the reverse operations are effected; namely, the rheostat handle is turned, without, however, pausing for the slacking of the armature speed until the current is entirely cut off the armature. The switch S, is then opened so as to cut off the motor fields, and the motor is thus entirely disconnected from the circuit. In some cases, when the speed of the motor has to be adjusted, a separate rheostat, called a *field rheostat*, is inserted in the circuit of the field coils C, C, and out of the path of the armature current. By altering the resistance in the field-magnet circuit, within proper limits, the current strength passing through these, being controlled by Ohm's law, will vary the amount of flux passing through the

THE TRANSMISSION OF POWER.   211

magnetic circuit including the armature, and force the latter to vary its speed in order to maintain a constant C. E. M. F.

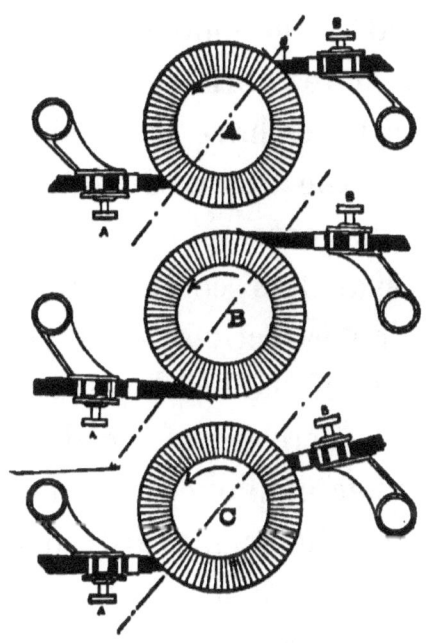

FIG. 58.—ADJUSTMENT OF BRUSHES ON A COMMUTATOR.

The correct position of a pair of brushes resting on a bipolar commutator is shown in Fig. 58 at A. If we suppose that this is the position of *sparkless commutation;* i.e., the position at which the brushes will pass current into the armature with the least sparking, then, as the load is gradually applied to the motor, and it performs more and more work, it is usually found that the brushes have to be shifted backward, or in the opposite direction to that in which the motor is moving, in order to preserve sparkless commutation. When the machine is acting as a generator, a *forward lead* of the brushes becomes necessary, with increase of load, as at B, whereas, when employed as a motor taking current from the mains, instead of supplying current to the mains, the lead of the brushes is *backward* as at C. In the most recent types of well designed motors, however, the sparking at the commutator is so slight at full load that no shifting of the brushes is necessary.

We have already referred to the *efficiency* of the motor; namely, to the ratio existing between the mechanical activity it develops at its pulley, and the electric activity it absorbs at its terminals. The losses which occur in the motor are all of a frictional nature, but may be divided into:

(1) Mechanical frictions.
(2) Magnetic frictions.
(3) Electric frictions.

Mechanical frictions are those which are produced at the bearings, brushes and in air churning. The magnetic frictions are those which occur during the rotation of the armature in the flux, and the consequent rapid reversal of the magnetism in its core. It is found that when iron has its magnetism reversed, there is a certain amount of energy expended in the iron at each reversal. The more powerful the magnetism the greater will be the expenditure of energy in every cubic centimetre or cubic inch of iron per reversal. The energy takes the form of heat, so that when we rapidly reverse the magnetic flux in a piece of iron or steel we heat it even though no friction in the mechanical sense occurs. This loss of energy by magnetic friction is called loss of energy by *hysteresis*, or *hysteretic loss of energy*. The more powerful the magnetic flux through the armature; the more rapid the rotation, and the greater the number of poles, the greater will be the hysteretic loss of energy. In a bipolar field, all the iron in the armature core reverses the direction of its magnetic flux twice in each revolution. In a quadripolar field it reverses four times in a revolution, and so on.

Thus, referring to Fig. 25, it will be

THE TRANSMISSION OF POWER. 215

observed that the armature A, is magnetized by the flux passing through it in the direction of the flux, having north polarity over the surface opposing the field pole S, where the flux emerges, and south polarity where the flux enters, over the surface opposite the field pole N. After the armature has made half a revolution, the direction of magnetism in its mass will be reversed, the part marked n, in the figure then becoming the part marked s, and *vice versa*. It is this reversal of magnetism which gives rise to hysteresis, and the more powerful the magnetic intensity in the armature which has to be reversed, the greater the hysteretic loss.

Electrical friction is due either to *eddy currents*, or *stray currents* set up by dynamo action in the mass of the conductor, armature core, or field poles; or, to the ordinary thermal expenditure of energy by the passage of the armature currents and field currents through their respective windings. If, for example, the field coils of a motor take a current of 3 amperes steadily, to excite them from mains at a pressure of 110 volts, then they will expend, in heating the field coils, an activity of 330 watts continuously.

CHAPTER VIII.

ELECTRIC TRANSMISSION OF POWER.

THE high efficiency, low cost, and comparative ease with which the electric motor can be controlled as to speed and power; the fact that it can be made to automatically regulate the current it requires; and its cleanliness, noiselessness, safety, compactness and portability, cause it to stand to-day in these respects unrivalled as a prime mover. Not only, however, does the electric motor possess these points of excellence far in excess of other prime movers, but it also possesses special advantages in the field of long distance transmission of power.

It will be interesting to discuss the electric motor in this respect and to examine the conditions under which power can be transmitted over considerable distances. Suppose, for example, that it is desired to furnish, at a distant point, a steady activity of 50 horse-power, for 10 hours a day. This power may be employed, for example, to drive the machinery in a factory. We can either put a steam engine in the factory, or install there an electric motor, drive a generator at some distant point, from a water-power or steam engine, and connect the generator with the motor by insulated electric conductors.

A system for the distribution of electric energy is represented in Fig. 59, where G, is the generator, situated at the source of power. M, is the motor at the factory, or point where the power is to be delivered, and *ab*, *cd*, are the wires connecting the two places. It is theoretically possible to employ only one wire, using the earth as a return conductor, as in telegraphy, but in practice, this arrangement has never been found satisfactory for the

Fig. 59.—Typical Electric Transmission System.

transmission of power, and two conductors are always employed.

The distance between *G* and *M*, the generator and motor, that is between the points of supply and delivery, may vary from a few feet to many miles. In factories, power is distributed from one building to another, or from different parts of the same building by means of belts and counter-shafting. The friction of such belts and shafts when long, may represent a considerable waste of power, so that it is often much more economical to restrict the counter-shafts to short lengths, each operated by a separate motor, and distribute the power from a single central source, or *power house*, to all these motors, as secondary centres of distribution. In such cases the transmission lines may be only a few hundred feet in length.

In cities, where electric central stations have been constructed, the demand for power, either for industrial or domestic uses, may be supplied by motors operated on electric circuits consisting of the street mains. In such cases, the distributing circuits may be one or two miles in length. Finally, cases may occur where power can be developed under specially economical advantages, at particular localities; as, for example, at a waterfall, where turbines are installed, and thus cheap power may be transmitted to a distant city at a cost which may be less than that of producing the power in that city by the steam engine. In some cases, the distance to which the power may be transmitted may be many miles.

Systems of electric transmission of power are, to-day, in fairly extended use. Moreover, this use is found in practice to be so satisfactory that it is rapidly increasing.

The greatest distance to which power has been electrically carried in any large quantity is 109 miles, which is the distance between the river Neckar at Lauffen, Germany, and the city of Frankfort. During the Frankfort Electric Exhibition of 1891, about 200 horse-power was steadily transmitted from turbines driven at Lauffen to the Exhibition Building at Frankfort.

The longest electric power transmission circuit operating commercially at the present day is at the San Joaquin valley to Fresno, Cal., over a distance of 35 miles, at an alternating-current pressure (triphase) of 11,200 volts between conductors. The next longest circuit in the United States is from Folsom to Sacramento, Cal., a distance of 24 miles, transmitting 3,000 HP. at 11,500 volts alternating triphase pressure. The longest circuit in Europe is from Tivoli to Rome, a distance of 18 miles at an alternating-current uniphase pressure of 5,000 volts. This system has been installed three years.

We propose to examine the conditions which affect the problem commercially. Assuming that the 50-horse-power continuous-current motor installed in the factory above referred to, may be wound for any desired pressure, and will possess, when so wound, an efficiency of 90 per cent., then the electric horse-power which must be supplied to its terminals, in order to maintain a steady mechanical activity, will be, $\frac{50}{0.9}$ = 55.55 horse-power = 55.55 × 746 = 41,440 watts = 41.44 KW. This electric activity could be supplied as 41,440 amperes at a pressure of 1 volt, in which case the motor would have to be wound for 1 volt; or, as 20,000 amperes at a pressure of 2.072 volts; or, as 1,000 amperes at a pressure of 41.44 volts; or, 100 amperes at a pressure of 414.4 volts; or, 10 amperes at a pressure of 4,144 volts. In each case, the motor would have to be wound for the required pressure.

Let us suppose that the cost of winding the motor is the same whatever pressure might be employed. This would not be strictly true, since the winding for either a very low pressure, or a very high pressure motor would be comparatively expensive; but, within a certain range, say from 50 volts to 1,000 volts, the cost would, probably, be nearly the same. Similarly, the cost of winding the generator for any pressure may be considered at present as constant. Let us also suppose that a certain loss of power is allowed in the transmission lines or conductors, say 10 per cent. of the full-load power developed at generator terminals. The efficiency of the line being, therefore, $\frac{9}{10}$, the power to be supplied at the generator terminals would be $\frac{41.44}{0.9} =$ 46.04 KW.

We then have an unwound generator at the transmitting end of the line, whose output, at full load, must be 46.04 KW, an unwound motor at the factory, or receiving end of the line, whose intake must be 41.44 KW, and whose output will be 50 horse-power, or 37.3 KW. The size of the conductors between these two points remains to be determined.

Let us suppose that the distance between these two stations is 5 miles; then the total length of circuit will be 10 miles, including the outgoing and returning conductors. In order that the loss of activity in the resistance of these 10 miles of conducting wire, shall as above assumed, be 10 per cent. of the activity supplied at the generator terminals, it is necessary that the drop of pressure produced by the working current in these 10 miles, shall be 10 per cent. of the pressure at the generator terminals. Thus, if the pressure at generator terminals be 500 volts, and the pressure at the motor terminals 450 volts, then the drop of pressure in the line will be 50 volts, or 10 per cent. of that at generator terminals, and the activity expended in heating the resistance of the line wires will be, in watts,

50 volts × working current in amperes, while the activity expended in the motor will be

450 volts × working current in amperes, the total activity of the generator, being,

500 volts × working current in amperes.

THE TRANSMISSION OF POWER. 227

If then, we wind the generator for 10 volts, and the motor for 9 volts, we lose 10 per cent. of our electric activity in the line, but the current must be $\frac{46,040}{10} = 4,604$ amperes, and the drop in the two lines together, one volt, or half a volt in each. The resistance of the two lines together must, therefore, be $\frac{1}{4,604}$ ohm, and the resistance per mile must be $\frac{1}{10}$th of this, or $\frac{1}{46,040}$ ohm. Ordinary trolley wire, No. 0 A. W. G., has a resistance of, approximately, half an ohm per mile. Consequently, the size of conductor, which would have to be employed in order to have only $\frac{1}{46,040}$ ohm per mile, would have to be $\frac{46,040}{2} = 23,020$ times as heavy, or as large in cross-section. Such an enormous conductor would be prohibitively costly and, therefore, such a system of transmission could not be carried out in practice.

If now, the generator were wound for 100 volts, and the motor for 90 volts, representing a drop in the transmission line of 10 volts, or 5 volts in each wire, the current strength in the circuit would be $\frac{46,040}{100} = 460.4$ amperes. The resistance of conductor, which would produce a drop of 10 volts with this current would be $\frac{10}{460.4}$ ohm = $\frac{1}{46.04}$ ohm, and this being the resistance of 10 miles of conductor, the resistance per mile should be $\frac{1}{460.4}$ ohm. If we assume the resistance of a trolley wire, as before, to be exactly half an ohm, the size of the conductor necessary would be equal to $\frac{460.4}{2} = 230.2$ trolley wires in cross-section or weight.

By increasing the pressure of transmission ten times; namely, from 10 volts to 100 volts, we have reduced by 100 times the size of wire, which is necessary in order to transmit a given activity of 50 horse-power with a fixed percentage of loss, because we have reduced the current strength ten times, and we have increased the permissible drop in the circuit from 1 volt to 10 volts, so that the resistance has been increased 100 times.

In the same way, if the generator be wound for 1,000 volts, and the motor for 900 volts, allowing 10 per cent. drop in transmission lines, as before, the current strength necessary to deliver 46,040 watts at the generator terminals will be $\frac{46,040}{1,000} = 46.04$ amperes, and the resistance which will have to exist in the two transmission lines, in order to produce with this current a drop of 100 volts, will be $\frac{100}{46.04} =$ 2.173 ohms; or, $\frac{2.173}{10} = 0.217$ ohm per mile. If we assume that the trolley wire has just 0.5 ohm per mile, then the size of the wire necessary to employ between the generator and motor will be $\frac{0.50}{0.2173} =$ 2.302 times that of trolley wire. Roughly speaking, therefore, the size of the wire would only be twice that of the trolley wire. That is, for a loss of 10 per cent. or 4.604 KW. in transmission the size of wire for

THE TRANSMISSION OF POWER. 231

10 volts at generator terminals, and 9 at motor terminals, would have to be 23,020 times trolley wire.

100 volts at generator terminals and 90 at motor terminals, 230.2 times trolley wire.

1,000 volts at generator terminals and 900 at motor terminals, 2.302 times trolley wire.

10,000 volts at generator terminals and 9,000 at motor terminals, 0.02303 times trolley wire.

In other words, the cost of copper required for a given distance and given loss in transmission varies inversely as the square of the electric pressure.

We have hitherto assumed that the distance between the generator and the motor was 5 miles. Let us now suppose that this distance is doubled, or changed to 10 miles, and that the length of the circuit is, consequently, changed to 20 miles. If, as before, 10 per cent. of the electric activity has to be expended in the resistance of the circuit, then the same number of volts drop will have to be developed in 20 miles, which previously were developed in 10, so that the resistance per mile of the conductor must be halved for any given pressure at generator and motor.

Thus, if the generator be wound for 1,000 volts and the motor for 900 volts, the drop in the transmission lines will be 100 volts, as before. The current will be 46.04 amperes, and the resistance of the circuit as before $\frac{100}{46.04} = 2.302$ ohms, and the resistance per mile, $\frac{1}{20}$th of this, or

THE TRANSMISSION OF POWER. 233

0.1151 ohm, requiring a wire $\dfrac{0.5}{0.1151} =$ 4.604 times that of trolley wire, or twice as big a wire as when the circuit was only 10 miles in length. Moreover, since we have to provide 20 miles of this double wire, instead of 10 miles, it is evident that the total weight of copper conductor will have increased four times.

Similarly, it will readily be found that if we trebled the distance between generator and motor we should have to use a wire three times as large for 30 miles as for 10 miles, and would, therefore, require 9 times the total weight of the copper needed in the first instance. In other words, the total weight of conductor required in a transmission system varies with the square of the distance between generator and motor for a given pressure of transmission, and for a given percentage of loss of activity. In order, therefore, to transmit power economically over considerable distance, it is essential to employ high electric pressures, since otherwise the cost of copper becomes prohibitive.

In building and winding continuous-current dynamo machines, whether for motors or generators, the limit of pressure which can be safely employed, depends upon the character of the insulation employed in the winding, and upon the nature of the commutator. The commutator is obviously a weak point in such machines, since the full electric pressure has to be maintained between the brushes which are only a few inches apart, and are separated by only a few strips of mica on a revolving cylinder. The highest electric pressures which are employed in dynamo machines are 10,000 volts. These pressures, however, are only employed in a few generators for series arc-light circuits and are not employed in motors. The highest pressures for which motors have been built, are practically 2,000 volts, while ordinarily 1,000 volts is the limit of pressure in motor construction. Consequently, under the conditions imposed by the art of motor building, as it exists to-day, the limitations of distance to which power can be transmitted by the continuous current are those which are prescribed either by the cost of conductor, or by the cost of power wasted in conductors at this limiting pressure of 1,000 volts. Moreover, at pressures exceeding this amount, the motors become dangerous to handle without precautions, since the shock from a thousand volt circuit is a serious one.

Assuming that the amount of money which must be expended in conductors to transmit a given number of horsepower over any actual distance, at, say 1,000 volts pressure, is not excessive; or, in other words, that it will pay to employ continuous-current electric transmission under these conditions, the question next arises, What should be the percentage of drop allowed in the line? If we employ a large percentage of drop we reduce the size and cost of the copper conductors, but at the same time we waste more activity in the conductors, which wasted activity has a money value. At what point then should the drop be fixed so as to secure the maximum economy?

In practice the solution to this problem can only be determined by making actual estimates with different percentages of drop. For example, if the distance between generator and motor be 1 mile, and the pressure at the generator terminals 1,000 volts, then the problem is to determine what shall be the most economical drop to employ in the line conductors. It is evident that the amount of power to be transmitted does not enter directly into this question, because, if we double the power transmitted, we merely double the whole transmission system, including generator, wires and motors, so that we may, for convenience, simply consider the transmission of one horse-power. Let us suppose that 1 KW capacity in motors costs say $40 when installed, so that 1,000 KW maximum mechanical delivery at the motor shaft costs $40,000 in motor machinery. Then, if the efficiency of the motor be taken, at say 90 per cent., which would be a fair value for moderately large sizes of motors, the electric activity at motor terminals, per KW delivery at belt, would be 1.111 KW. If now, a size of wire which would expend in resistance at the working pressure 10 per cent. of the maximum pressure employed, the total activity at the generator terminals would be 1.235 KW and the power delivered to the generator shaft assuming 90 per cent. efficiency would be $\frac{1.235}{0.9}$ KW = 1.372 KW. Consequently, we have, under these conditions, to supply 1.372 KW to the generator shaft in order to obtain 1 KW from the motor shaft. The total annual charge of the system will be the interest and depreciation on the investment, added to the cost of superintendence and repairs and the cost of the power supplied at the generator shaft. If the power be obtained from a waterfall, which is not limited in supply, then a little extra loss of power in the line will not be a matter of serious consequence, since it will only involve the use of a correspondingly larger generator and turbine, so that the cost will only be increased by the fixed charges on the extra investment. If, however, the power to be transmitted is from a steam plant, not only will the engines and boilers and generators at the transmitting end have to be larger, by reason of a greater waste of power in the line, but also the coal consumed at the generating end will be increased. We, have, therefore, to find by trial and estimate such a size of wire as will make the total annual cost of the power delivered a minimum. If we make the wire too small and its resistance too great, its first cost will be reduced and the annual interest on the wire will be reduced. There will practically be no depreciation on copper wire, although there will be some depreciation on the poles, supports or insulation which must be maintained about the wire. On the other hand, the engines, boilers and generators will cost more, and the coal per horse-power hour, or per KW hour, delivered will cost more. If we make the wire too large, we reduce the cost of coal in the generating station, and also the fixed annual charges of interest, depreciation, superintendence and repairs on generating plant which is now smaller, but we have an increase in the fixed charges upon the greater investment in the line conductors. Economy requires that the total charges or total annual expense shall be as small as possible, and, consequently, the size of the wire must be so chosen that under the estimated conditions of load the total cost of wire, power and generating apparatus shall be a minimum.

CHAPTER IX.

ALTERNATING-CURRENT MOTORS.

CONSIDERABLE attention has been paid of recent years to the development of alternating-current machinery, owing to the facilities which such machinery possesses for the long-distance transmission of power. While it will be necessary to refer briefly to the differences between the alternating and continuous current, space will not permit the discussion of the peculiarities of alternating currents to any great length, and the reader is therefore referred to the authors' volume on "Alternating Electric Currents," in the Elementary Electro-Technical Series, for more complete particulars in that direction.

A *continuous E. M. F.*, that is an E. M. F. which always acts in the same direction, establishes, or tends to establish, a continuous electric current in its circuit. *An alternating E. M. F.*, that is an E. M. F. which at regular successive in-intervals reverses its direction, establishes, or tends to establish, an *alternating current* in its circuit. A continuous-current circuit has its analogue in a reservoir, which discharges through a pipe or hydraulic conductor. An alternating-current circuit has its analogue in a hydraulic circuit in which a pump drives water alternately backwards and forwards at regular intervals. The tidal flow in a river is another example of alternating water currents.

A complete to-and-fro motion or double alternation constitutes a *cycle*. The number of cycles per second, or per minute, constitutes what is called the *frequency*. In commercial practice the frequency varies between 25 cycles per second, or 50 reversals of E. M. F. and current per second, (1,500 cycles per minute, or 3,000 reversals or alternations per minute) and 140 cycles, or 280 alternations per second, (8,400 cycles, or 16,800 alternations per minute).

The current strength in an alternating-current circuit, unlike that in a continuous-current circuit, does not depend only upon the E. M. F. and the resistance as related by Ohm's law. To determine the current strength in alternating-current circuits, it is necessary to take into account a new quantity called *reactance*. Reactance is a quantity similar to resistance, and like it, is capable of being expressed in ohms. Its value increases directly with the frequency. A coil of wire, for example, either with or without an iron core, having a resistance of 3 ohms, will permit a current of 3 1/3 amperes to flow through it under a continuous pressure of 10 volts; but, if the E. M. F. applied to its terminals, instead of being continuous, alternates with a frequency of say 50 cycles per second, the coil will possess not only a resistance of 3 ohms, but a reactance which might be, at this frequency, say 4 ohms. This reactance has to be considered as to its effect of reducing the current strength. If the frequency were doubled; that is, increased to 100 cycles per second, or 200 reversals of E. M. F. and current per second, the reactance would be doubled, or increased to 8 ohms, and if the frequency were made 150 cycles per second, the reactance would be increased to 12 ohms.

THE TRANSMISSION OF POWER. 245

The amount of the reactance depends not only upon the number of turns in the coil but also on their ability to produce magnetic flux through the coil. The greater amount of magnetic flux which will be produced by the current in passing through the coil, the greater will be the reactance of the coil for a given frequency. The reactance is sometimes described as the *choking effect* of the current, since it tends to check or choke the current which flows; but the amount of this choking, that is the *total effective resistance*, cannot be determined by simply adding together the resistance and reactance. Thus, in the case of the above coil, having 3 ohms resistance and 4 ohms reactance, at a frequency of 50 cycles per second, generally represented thus, 50~, the effective resistance of the coil will not be 7 ohms, but can be obtained by drawing the resistance as the base, and the reactance as the perpendicular of a right-angled triangle as in Fig. 60. The combined influence of reactance and resistance will then be repre-

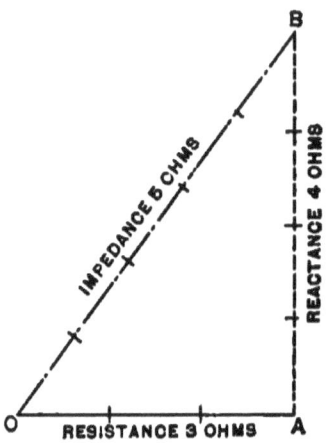

Fig. 60.—Diagrams Indicating Relation of Impedance to Resistance and Reactance.

sented by the length of the hypothenuse OB, which in this case will be 5 ohms, so that the current strength passing through the circuit will be 10 volts, divided by 5 ohms = 2 amperes.

THE TRANSMISSION OF POWER. 247

Ohm's law, as modified for alternating current circuits, is, therefore,

$$\text{Amperes} = \frac{\text{Volts E. M. F.}}{\text{Ohms Impedance.}}$$

If the frequency of alternation be doubled, so that the reactance is doubled, or becomes 8 ohms, the *impedance*, as shown in Fig. 61, will be increased to 8.544 ohms, and the current strength in the coil will, therefore, be reduced to $\frac{10}{8.544} = 1.17$ amperes. If the frequency of alternation were made indefinitely small, so that the current became continuous, the impedance would become the simple resistance.

Reactance plays a prominent part in all alternating-current circuits. It is usefully employed in apparatus called *alternating-current transformers*, which consist essentially of coils of wire wound upon a common core. One of these coils is connected with the *driving* or *primary circuit*,

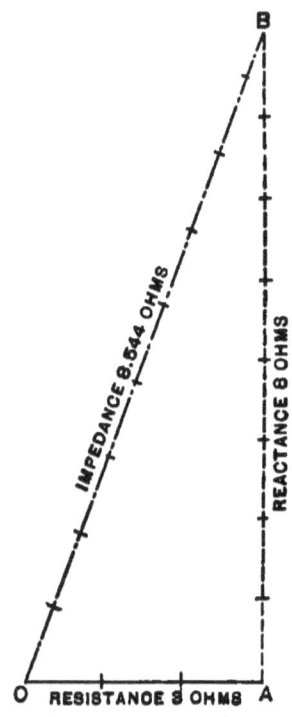

Fig. 61.—Diagram Indicating Relation of Impedance to Reactance.

while the other coil is connected with the *driven* or *secondary circuit*; i. e., the circuit to which the activity has to be transferred. When the secondary circuit is opened and is, therefore, devoid of activity, the reactance of the coil in the primary circuit has a maximum value depending upon the frequency, the number of turns, and their arrangement upon the iron core, so that the impedence of the primary coil has a definite and usually a large value in ohms. Consequently, the primary coil takes a very small current when supplied at a given pressure. When, however, the secondary circuit is closed through incandescent lamps, motors, or other devices, the effect of the activity, which is thus transferred from the primary to the secondary coil is to lower the reactance of the primary coil, and thus reduce its impedance, permitting a greater current strength and activity to enter the primary coil from its supply mains.

An alternating-current transformer is, therefore, an apparatus, which, without revolving parts, automatically transfers energy from its primary to its secondary circuit. At the same time, it possesses a very valuable property of transforming the energy, in regard to pressure and current, in a manner depending upon the winding of the primary and secondary coils. If the primary and secondary coils have the same size and the same number of turns, the primary and secondary E. M. F.'s will be practically the same, but if the primary winding has, say 10 times the number of turns as in the secondary winding, the E. M. F. acting in the secondary circuit will be $\frac{1}{10}$th of that in the primary circuit. Such a transformer is called a *step-down transformer*, because the pressure is reduced in the secondary circuit. If, however, the secondary winding has, say 10 times the number of turns as in the primary winding, the secondary E. M. F. will be 10 times as great as the primary E. M. F. and the current strength will be, approximately, $\frac{1}{10}$th of the primary current strength. Such a transformer is called a *step-up transformer*, because it effects an increase in pressure in its driving circuit.

It is obvious, that if no activity were absorbed in a transformer, the activity in the secondary circuit would be equal to the activity received by the transformer at its primary terminals. As a matter of fact, the loss in a transformer, although comparatively small, is nevertheless quite appreciable. A large transformer will deliver, at its secondary terminals, about 98 per cent. of the activity it receives at its primary terminals, or will absorb as heat, about 2 per cent. of its maximum received activity. This loss of 2 per cent. will be only slightly reduced at no load, or on open secondary circuit, so that, if a 10 KW transformer; *i. e.*, a transformer capable of delivering steadily an activity of 10 KW in its secondary circuit, absorbs 300 watts at full load, it will require to be supplied with 10.3 KW at its primary terminals, and its efficiency will be $\frac{10}{10.3} =$ 97.09 per cent. Usually, the greater part of this loss of 300 watts will occur at all loads, so that roughly say 200 watts will have to be expended in operating the transformer, when it is delivering no power to its secondary circuit; *i. e.*, when its secondary circuit is open.

We have seen that in a continuous-current circuit the activity is always expressed as the product of the amperes and the volts, or in other words, on the rate of supply of current, and the pressure at which that current is supplied. In an alternating-current circuit, however, this relation ceases, as a general rule, to be strictly applicable. This is for the reason that the impulses, or waves of current, do not, as a rule, exactly coincide with the impulses or waves of E. M. F. When the current waves do coincide, or keep exactly in step with the E. M. F. waves, then the activity, in watts, is the product of the amperes and the volts, as in continuous-current circuits, but it usually happens that the current waves do not coincide, or are out of step with, the E. M. F. in the circuit, and generally lag behind the latter. If we could watch the waves of E. M. F. and current, we should find that the crests of the E. M.

F. waves usually arrived ahead of the current waves, although under certain circumstances the reverse may be true, and the current wave crests may arrive in advance of the E. M. F. wave crests. The current in these cases is described as *lagging* or *leading* respectively.

The effect of a lag or a lead is to produce an opposition between the E. M. F. and the current which it drives, since it is evident, that during the entire cycle, the E. M. F. will not be in the same direction as the current, but during a portion of the cycle, the current and the E. M. F. waves will have opposite directions. For this reason the activity of the E. M. F. will not be so great as the product of the volts and the amperes, but will have to be reduced by a factor called the *power factor*, always less than unity, and only reaching

THE TRANSMISSION OF POWER. 255

unity when there is no lag or lead; *i. e.*, when current and E. M. F. waves coincide. In special cases the power factor may be as low as say 1 per cent., in which case the current and the pressure would be nearly out of step, the crests of one nearly coinciding with the mean levels of the other. Under ordinary circumstances, the power factor is usually more than 50 per cent. or 0.5, and it is quite commonly over 90 per cent. or 0.9. In such cases we have to multiply the volts by the amperes and by the power factor, in order to obtain the true activity. In other words, the volts and the amperes, when multiplied together, cannot be less and will generally be more than the actual activity of the circuit in which they are measured.

When a circuit has very small reactance, relatively to its resistance, the power factor will be large, or nearly 100 per cent. On the contrary, when the reactance is large relatively to the resistance, the power factor will be small. Consequently, the power factor of an incandescent lamp is almost exactly 100 per cent., because the filament, having only a single bend or loop, possesses an extremely small reactance and a relatively large resistance. Therefore, if we multiply the volts and the amperes observed at the terminals of an incandescent lamp, or group of incandescent lamps supplied on an alternating-current circuit, we obtain almost exactly the real activity which is supplied to them. If, however, we take a coil of wire having a large number of turns and a small resistance, the pressure and current, observed at the terminals of this coil, may be considerably out of step, or may be, as it is frequently called, *displaced in phase*, so that the product of the volts and amperes may be considerably in excess of the real activity expended in the coil.

FIG. 62.—ALTERNATING-CURRENT DYNAMO.

Any dynamo for generating alternating E. M. F.'s is called an *alternator*. Fig. 62, represents an alternator employed for electric lighting. Since every dynamo-electric generator develops in its armature E. M. F.'s which alternate, it is evident that a continuous-current machine differs from an alternator principally in the fact that it employs a commutator to direct all the alternating-current impulses in the same direction, so far as the external circuit is concerned. In Fig. 62, is shown a sextipolar machine, driven by a pulley P, and provided with a pair of *collector rings* r, r, for delivering the alternating E. M. F. to the external circuit. The machine also drives by the pulley P_1, a small continuous-current generator G, called the *exciter*, the function of which is to produce a sufficiently powerful continuous current to excite the field-magnet coils M, M, M, of the alternator.

When two ordinary alternators are connected by a pair of wires, with the object of employing one as a generator and the other as a motor, it is found that the motor will not start from rest when connected to the running generator. This is for the reason that before the armature of the motor has had time to start up at full speed in one direction, by the action of any particular wave of current, the next and opposite wave of current has reversed the electro-dynamic force and arrested the motion. If, however, the motor armature be brought, by an externally applied force, up to the speed at which it should run in order to develop the same frequency as the generator, then if its field magnets are excited, its armature circuit may be closed in such a manner that the armature will fall into step with the impulses received from the generator, and the motor will commence to be driven. This is because the armature of the motor reverses the direction of its C. E. M. F. nearly in synchronism with the reversal of the direction of the current. The two machines then keep in step, or are said to run synchronously. The motor may exert a powerful torque and exert a considerable mechanical activity; but, provided that it be not too heavily overloaded, it will maintain its synchronism with the generator. On being subjected to an excessive load, it will fall out of step, will fail to receive activity from the generator, and will then rapidly come to rest.

The practical difficulty experienced with alternating-current motors, until recent times, was that they would not start from rest, so that a prime mover of some kind was necessary in order to bring the alternating-current motor up to speed before it could be usefully connected with the circuit. Synchronous alternating-current motors of this type have been brought up to speed in a variety of ways. In some cases, this is effected by means of special windings on the armature, capable of acting as continuous-current machines under light loads, and sometimes by storage batteries and auxiliary motors. In other cases continuous-current exciters are employed at each end of the line, as ordinary continuous-current generators and motors, thus obtaining sufficient power from the line circuit from the generating exciter to the motor exciter, to be able to run the motor armature unloaded, up to synchronous speed when the exciters would be disconnected from the circuit and the alternating-current armatures connected thereto. The inconvenience, however, of having to bring the motor armature up to speed, where frequent stoppages are necessary, becomes so great that the synchronous alternating-current motors have never come into extended commercial use. A device, however, which is sometimes used, is to provide the motor-armature with a double winding, one winding having a commutator for the production of continuous currents, and the other winding arranged, like that of an alternator armature, for the passage of alternating currents. By connecting the continuous-current winding with the alternating-current mains, the motor may be started and brought up to speed by allowing the field magnets to reverse their polarity at each alternation of the current, so that the magnetic flux reverses coincidently in both field and armature at every alternation of current. After full speed has been attained, the alternating-current winding is connected to the circuit, so that the

THE TRANSMISSION OF POWER.

motor runs synchronously, while the continuous-current winding supplies the current necessary to steadily energize the field magnets.

The difficulty of starting and operating synchronous alternating-current motors, has, however, led to the introduction and development of multiphase alternating-currents and multiphase motors.

A *multiphase alternating-current* system is a system of two or more circuits traversed by independent alternating currents, possessing a definite difference of phase.

A *diphase system*, or two-phase system, is a system consisting of circuits having two alternating currents differing in phase by one quarter of a cycle.

A *triphase system*, or three-phase system, is a system of circuits having three alternating currents, differing in phase by one-third of a cycle.

Multiphase systems of any complexity may exist, but in practice not more than three separate currents are employed.

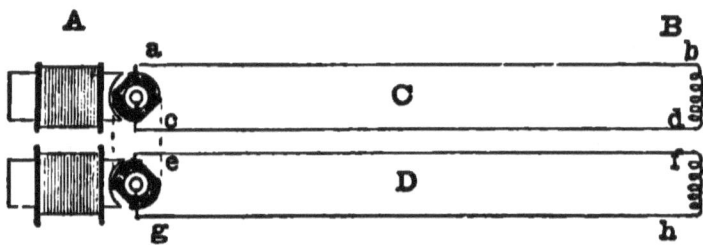

Fig. 63.—Diagram of Diphase System with Four Conductors.

Fig. 63, represents the simplest form of diphase system, comprising two distinct circuits supplied with alternating currents from a common source at *A*. The circuit *ab, cd*, taken by itself is a simple alternating-current circuit. The circuit *ef, gh*, taken similarly is also a simple alternating-current circuit, but these circuits, taken

THE TRANSMISSION OF POWER. 265

together, constitute a *diphase system*, for the reason that the waves of E. M. F. and current generated in the circuit *abcd*, differ in phase by one quarter of a cycle from those generated in the circuit *efgh*. The impulses reach their crests in one circuit, when at their zero or mean levels in the neighboring circuit. This result may be obtained by employing either two ordinary or uniphase generators, rigidly coupled together on the same shaft, in such a position that the E. M. F. waves in one are generated one quarter cycle ahead of the E. M. F. waves in the other; or, by employing two windings on the armature of one alternator so arranged as to produce the necessary difference in phase.

Instead of employing two entirely separate circuits for the two alternating currents of a diphased system, as shown in Fig. 63, a common return conductor may be employed and only three wires used as in Fig. 64. In such cases, the third, or middle conductor, is made about 40 per cent.

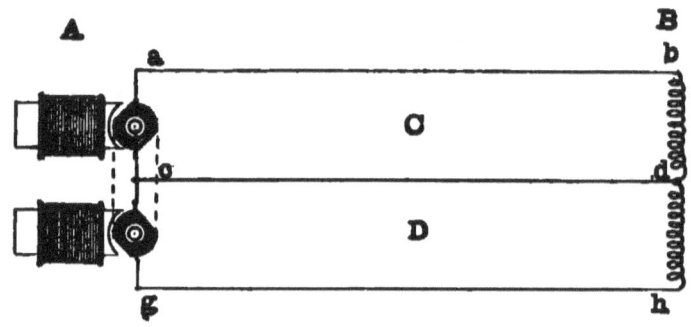

Fig. 64.—Diagram of Diphase System with Three Conductors.

heavier in order to carry the increased current strength. The diphase system requires that the waves of current and E. M. F. in the conductors $a\ b\ d$, shall be a quarter cycle out of step with those in the conductor $g\ h\ d$.

A *triphaser* is an alternator which produces three E. M. Fs. differing from one another in phase by one third of a cycle. Such triphase currents might be produced by three uniphase armatures rigidly

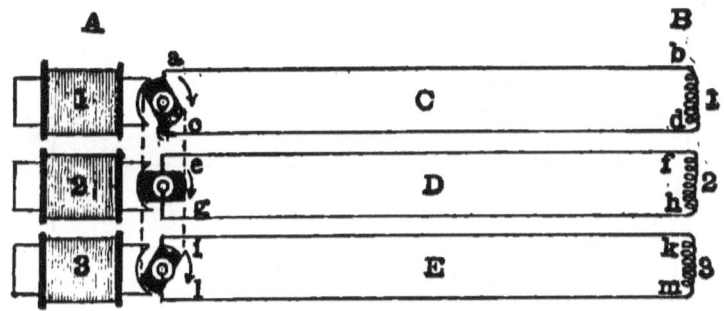

Fig. 65.—Triphase Six-Wire System.

clamped together on a single shaft, but so set that the E. M. Fs. differ in phase by one third of a complete cycle. Such a combination is diagrammatically represented in Fig. 65, where the three separate circuits have uniphase currents, but the current waves in the three circuits differ by one third of a cycle. In practice, however, six wires are never used for a triphaser, but three wires only, each wire serving in turn as the return of the other two. This arrangement is represented in Fig. 66.

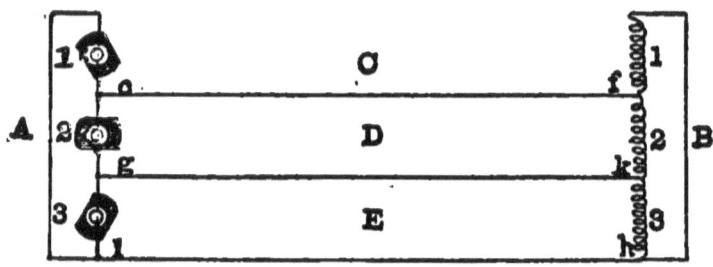

Fig. 66.—Triphase Three-Wire System.

Fig. 67, shows a form of triphaser having 40 poles and capable of maintaining an activity of 500 KW; 166 2/3 KW in each of its three circuits. The pressure is 500 volts between each pair of terminals. The armature is driven at 108 revolutions per minute. The frequency is 36~ per second. The dimensions of this machine are

THE TRANSMISSION OF POWER.

Fig. 67.—Three-Phase Alternator, 40 Poles, 500 KW.

107″ × 213″ and its height 150″. The total weight is 108,000 pounds, or about 216 pounds per KW of output. The armature has three separate windings in which triphase E. M. Fs. are developed. The three main leads are shown in the figure.

Fig. 68, shows another form of belt-driven triphaser, having 10 poles and making 600 revolutions per minute. The frequency is 50~ per second, the activity 250 KW; or, 83 1/3 KW, in each circuit. This machine is seen to be separately excited. Its weight is about 30,000 pounds, or 120 pounds per KW.

Another type of multiphase system is the *monocyclic system*. This system has been designed for use in central stations where the main load is that of lighting,

Fig. 68.—Three-Phase Alternator, 10 Poles, 250 KW.

but where alternating-current motors require to be operated from the circuit. The armature is wound with two sets of coils, one constituting the main winding, which corresponds to that of an ordinary uniphaser, while the second winding is of smaller cross-section and fewer turns, and is connected to the centre of the main winding as shown in Fig. 69, at A, where $a\ o\ b$, represents the main armature winding, and $o\ c$, the short coil or *teaser winding*. Three terminals are thus led out from the the armature at a, b and c. The terminals a and b, connected by means of collector rings and brushes to the external circuit, constitute the lighting circuit, while a third wire from c, enables an alternating-current motor to be operated in conjunction with the other two. The windings are so arranged that the E. M. F. in $C\ D$, is in diphase relation to that in $A\ B$, as rep-

THE TRANSMISSION OF POWER. 273

resented diagrammatically at B, in Fig. 69, the loop *a o b*, being wound on the drum at right angles to the half loop *o c*.

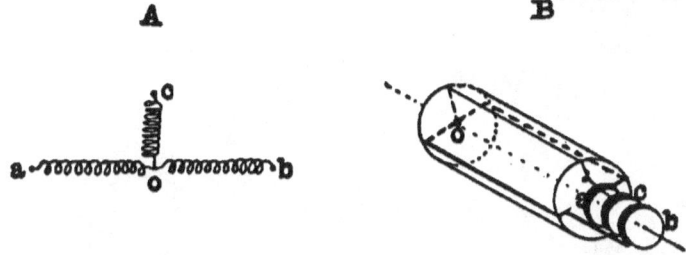

FIG. 69.—DIAGRAMS OF MONOCYCLIC ARMATURE WINDING.

A *monocyclic armature* is represented in Fig. 70. A, B and C, are the three col-

FIG. 70.—MONOCYCLIC ARMATURE.

lector rings, forming the main terminals of the armature. The windings are just visible in the slots left between the teeth or iron armature projections. The shape of the coils is represented in Fig. 71. The main coils are flat, while the teaser coils

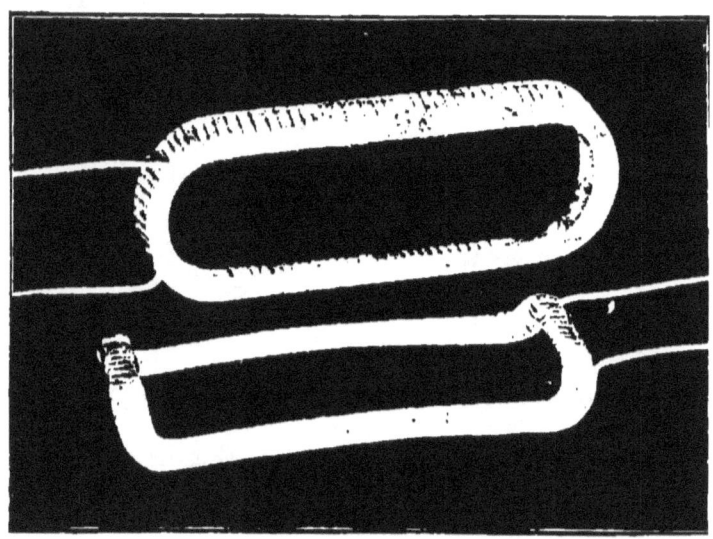

FIG. 71.—MAIN AND TEASER COILS.

are bent in such a manner as to permit them to be laid across the main coils in a midway position, so as to generate their E. M. Fs. a quarter cycle out of step with those in the main coils.

A form of *monocyclic alternator* is represented in Fig. 72. This is a 120 KW

Fig. 72.—Monocyclic Alternator, 40 Poles, 120 KW.

machine, wound for 60~ per second, and a pressure of 1,150, 2,300 or 3,450 volts between the main terminals, according to requirements. This machine weighs about 15,000 pounds or 125 pounds per KW.

The connections for use with a *monocyclic system* are shown in Fig. 73. Here the generator terminals A and B, are connected with the mains for lighting. T_3, represents a step-down transformer whose primary terminals P_1 and P_2, are connected to the mains A and B, respectively, at a pressure, of say 2,200 volts. The secondary terminals s_1, s_2 and s_3, of this transformer constitute a *uniphase three-wire system*, having 220 volts between s_1 or s_3 or 110 volts between s_1 and s_2; and 110 volts between s_2 and s_3, without any difference in phase. This is obtained by dividing the secondary coil into halves. The secondary circuit is connected with lamps on each side of the three-wire system as shown. T_4, is a step-down trans-

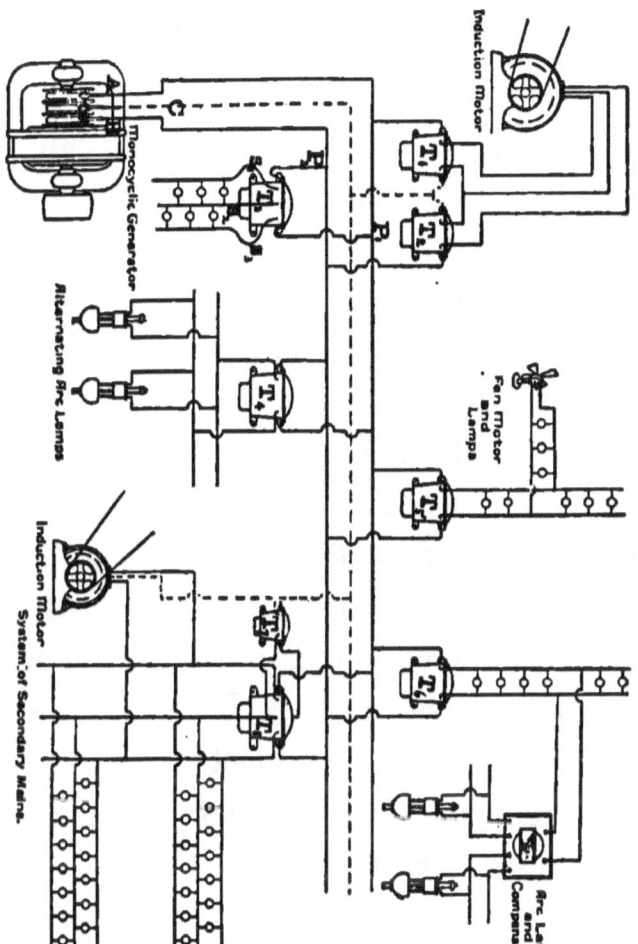

FIG. 73.—DISTRIBUTION BY MONOCYCLIC SYSTEM.

former, transforming from 2,200 to say, 50 volts, for operating two arc lamps in parallel. The primary terminals of this transformer are connected to the main leads A and B. T'_5, is a transformer whose primary terminals are also connected with A and B, while the secondary coil in this case, having a single pair of terminals, is connected directly with incandescent lamps, and also with a small fan motor, which being of small size can be operated without the use of multiphase currents. T_6, is also a uniphase transformer connected with the primary mains A and B, and feeding in its secondary circuit 110-volt lamps, as well as two arc lamps through a compensator.

Hitherto we have simply examined the devices which have been operated from the mains A and B, without the use of

THE TRANSMISSION OF POWER. 279

the *power wire*, the dotted line connected with the terminal C, and all that we have yet examined might have been obtained from an ordinary uniphaser. To operate an *induction motor*, two transformers have to be employed, such as T'_1 and T'_2, the primary terminals of one being connected between A and C, and those of the other between B and C. The secondary terminals, when connected with the motor, as shown, generate a system of triphase currents in the motor a. Similarly, the two transformers T'_7 and T'_8, one connected with its primary terminals between A and B, and the other transformer connected with its terminals between C, and the centre of the primary in T_8, produce in their secondary circuits a system of triphase E. M. Fs. and currents, capable of operating the induction motor as well as the incandescent lamps.

A *monocycler*, therefore, produces a uniphase main E. M. F. in its main circuit, which is employed for all uniphase purposes, such as lighting, or for the operation of synchronous motors. It also generates in a subsidiary, or auxiliary coil, an E. M. F. in diphase relation with the main E. M. F. and, by combining these two diphase E. M. Fs. through the connection of the third wire, triphase E. M. Fs. can be produced in the secondary circuits of suitably connected transformers.

Fig. 74, shows the connections employed for the distributing circuit of a triphaser. Here any pair of conductors may be regarded as an independent uniphase circuit, from which step-down transformers for uniphase work may be operated. Thus T_1, T_2 and T_3 are step-down transformers, each connected with one pair of high-pressure wires. A pair of transformers, however, operated from any two of the three, as shown at t_1 and t_2, will produce in their secondary circuits, when united in the manner represented, a triphase system of

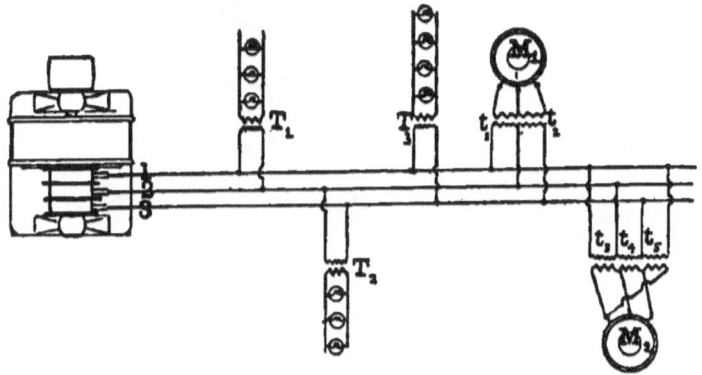

Fig. 74.—Connections of Triphase System.

E. M. Fs. and currents suitable for operating a triphase alternating-current motor M_1, but three transformers may also be employed, each connected across a pair of high-pressure wires as shown at t_3, t_4 and t_5. Their secondary circuits are connected with the three terminals of the triphase induction motor M_2.

Fig. 75, similarly represents the connections of a diphaser. Here two independ-

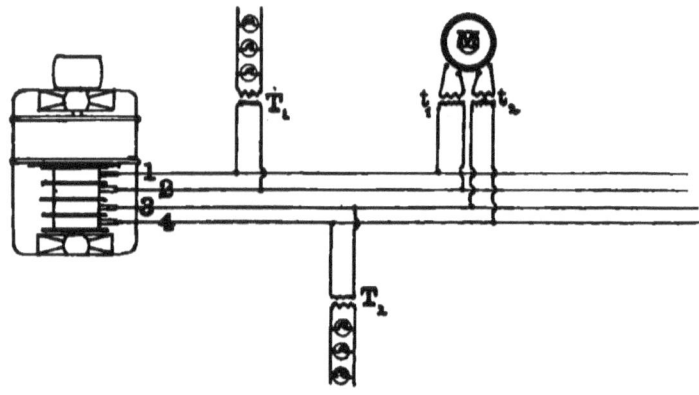

Fig. 75.—Connections of Diphase System.

ent circuits are shown, each of which may be treated as a *uniphase circuit*, as seen at T_1 and T_2. By operating two transformers, one from each circuit and connecting their secondaries together, as shown at t_1 and t_2, a diphase system of E. M. Fs.

and currents may be obtained, capable of operating a *diphase motor* M. As already pointed out three wires are theoretically sufficient for the operation of this system.

The triphase system of three wires possesses a distinct saving in copper over an ordinary uniphase, or a diphase system, for a given maximum pressure between any pair of conductors and a given percentage of drop in the lines. The saving in copper amounts to 25 per cent. of that required for a four-wire diphase, or a two-wire uniphase system.

CHAPTER X.

ROTATING MAGNETIC FIELDS.

It now remains to explain the manner in which a multiphase alternating-current motor operates when its stationary, or stator coils, are traversed by multiphase currents.

Let us suppose that a field frame is arranged with four poles and four coils, as shown in Fig. 76. Let coils 1 and 3, be joined together in series in one circuit, and coils 2 and 4, be also joined together in series in another circuit; moreover, let these two circuits be connected to the two windings of a diphaser; then, when one circuit has its full current strength, the

THE TRANSMISSION OF POWER. 285

other circuit will have no current passing through it. Let us suppose that at the interval of time represented at A, Fig. 76,

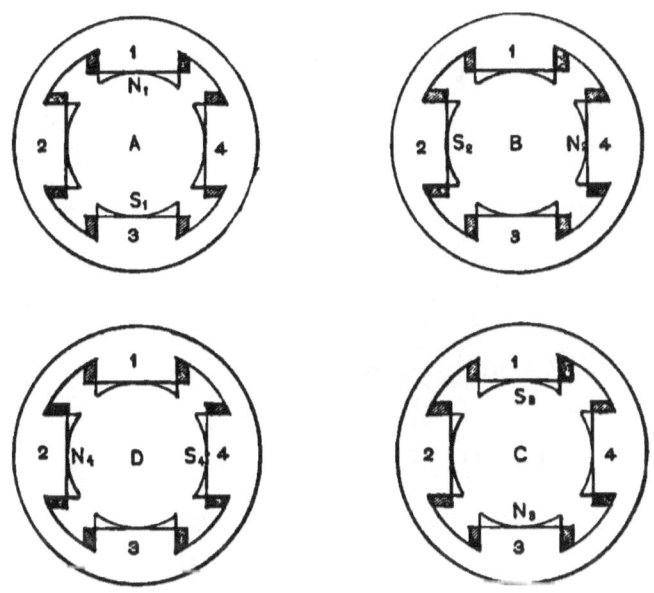

FIG. 76.—DIAGRAM ILLUSTRATING A ROTATING MAGNETIC FIELD.

coils 1 and 3, are receiving a wave of current which produces a north pole at 1, and a south pole at 3. At this instant there will be no current in the coils 2 and 4. A small compass needle, pivoted at the centre of the field frame, would, therefore, point to pole 3.

Next suppose, that a quarter cycle elapses, as at B; then the current in the coils 1 and 3, will have disappeared, and the current in 2 and 4, will have attained its maximum strength. Under these conditions, a north pole will be developed at 4, and a south pole at 2, so that the compass needle will have to rotate through 90°, and will now point to 2. Again, at the next quarter cycle represented at C, the current in 2 and 4, will have died away, but the current in 1 and 3, will have the opposite direction to that at A; that is to say, if A, represents the effect of the positive wave C, represents the effect of the negative wave. A north pole will, therefore, be formed at 3, and a south pole

THE TRANSMISSION OF POWER. 287

at 1. The compass needle will, therefore be rotated to 1, having described 180°. Again, *D*, represents the condition at the next quarter cycle, when the current flows through 2 and 4, producing a north pole at 2, and a south pole at 4. The needle will now be pointing to 4, and will have rotated through 270°. Finally, after a complete cycle has elapsed the condition at *A*, will be reproduced, when the needle will have completed a revolution. It is evident that the effect of the diphase currents in the field frame has been to produce a rotation of the magnetism of the field, in obedience to which the compass needle rotates once to each complete cycle.

If the frequency in the circuits be, say 50 cycles per second, the compass needle may be expected to make 50 complete revolutions per second, and would constitute a diminutive moving part or rotor. We have explained the successive steps of this rotating field that occur in Fig. 76, on the supposition that they take place in positions 90° apart. In practice, however, motors are frequently so constructed that the magnetic field rotates almost uniformly around the frame, instead of by jumps.

The motor constituted by the field frame and the rotating compass needle would obviously be very feeble. Magnetic action, however, may be intensified in various ways, either by employing a larger or more powerful compass needle, such, for example, as a suitably pivoted electromagnet, or, by employing a mass of iron for the rotating part, wound with coils of wire forming closed circuits, so that the moving or rotating magnetic field may induce in these coils powerful currents, whose magnetic flux will be attracted by the rotating field, thus turning the armature around.

There are thus two classes of multiphase motors, both of which employ a rotating field. In one class the rotating field acts upon a magnetized armature, which, after being set in rotation, keeps in step or in synchronism with the rotating field. In the other class, the rotating field acts so as to induce currents in the armature by the difference of speed between the rotating field and the rotating armature, so that the armature never quite attains the speed of the field, and lags behind it by an amount sometimes called the *slip*, which depends upon the torque or load. The first class embraces what are called *synchronous multiphase motors;* the second class, are called *induction multiphase motors*, or simply *induction motors*.

There is a marked difference between synchronous multiphase motors and synchronous uniphase motors. The latter are incapable of starting under ordinary practical conditions, since the magnetic field produced by a uniphase current does not rotate, but merely oscillates to-and-fro. The former are so designed as to be capable of self-starting, owing to the influence of the rotating magnetic field, which pulls the armature around with it. If one of the diphase circuits of the field frame be reversed it will be found that the effect is to reverse the direction of rotation of the field and, therefore, the direction of rotation of the armature.

Fig. 77 represents diagrammatically the action of a *triphase rotating field*. Here six poles 1, 2, 3, 4, 5 and 6, are represented, with their coils so arranged that 1 and 4, are

THE TRANSMISSION OF POWER.   291

in series in one circuit, and 2 and 5, in series in the second circuit, and 3 and 6, in series in the third circuit. Six conditions

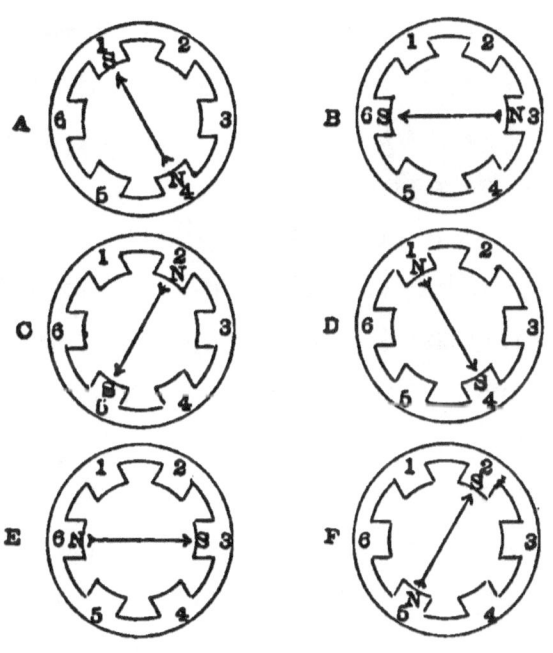

FIG. 77.—DIAGRAM OF TRIPHASE ROTATING FIELD.

are represented at A, B, C, D, E, and F, during successive sixths of one complete cycle. At A, the compass needle is shown pointing to pole 1, the current being a maximum in coils 1 and 4. At *B*, the needle is shifted to pole 6, the current being now a maximum in coils 3 and 6. Similarly, at each successive sixth of a period, the needle will have shifted around one-sixth of the revolution as the current successively rises and falls in different circuits. It will be seen that the difference between a *diphase field frame*, and a *triphase field frame*, consists in the number and arrangement of the coils, but that the effect is otherwise the same, the result of combining the effects of successive current waves being to produce a *rotary magnetism*. The armature, as before, may be of the synchronous, or of the induction type. It will be readily understood that Fig. 77 is diagrammatic only. The actual rotation of the field being usually obtained by a somewhat different winding.

A synchronous multiphase motor has the same speed at all loads. If overloaded it will come to rest, but will start again from rest when the load is removed. An induction motor will very nearly reach the full rotary speed of the field at light load, but will be retarded, or will slip, as already mentioned, at full load. The amount of slip is comparatively small, being only about 3 per cent. in large motors, and about 5 per cent. in small motors. Induction motors may be designed which will start from rest under a very powerful torque. It is usually necessary, especially with large motors, to insert resistances into the armature circuit at starting, in order to check the very powerful currents which tend to be developed in them when started from rest; for, since the E. M. Fs. induced in the armature are proportional to the difference in speed between the armature and the rotary field, it is evident that when just starting this difference of speed will be a maximum, and the current will be very powerful, producing reactionary effects that are disadvantageous. The effect of inserting resistance in the armature circuit is to check the strength of these currents and so improve the starting torque of the motor.

A form of triphase motor, of 15-horsepower capacity, is represented in Fig. 78. The three main terminals are seen at A, B, and C. The field frame F, is of laminated iron. W, is a portion of the field winding. The lever L, is provided for the purpose of starting the motor effectively. When the lever is in the position shown, resistances are left in the armature circuit as above described, so as to obtain, when starting, a more powerful and less wasteful torque,

THE TRANSMISSION OF POWER. 295

and a reduced current in the armature coils, which are hidden from view. As soon as the armature has come up to speed,

FIG. 78.—MULTIPHASE INDUCTION MOTOR.

the lever L, is pushed in toward the armature, thereby bringing a metal collar into contact with the strips S, thus short-circuiting the resistance, and improving the action of the motor for full speed. In order to

296   THE ELECTRIC MOTOR AND

reverse the direction of motion of the armature, it is sufficient to reverse any pair

FIG. 79.—HOIST, WITH 10 KILOWATT MULTIPHASE MOTOR.

of wires on the terminals A, B and C. This has the effect of reversing the direction of the rotating field. By examining the figure, it will be seen that the dimensions of this motor are relatively very small as indicated by the foot rule that lies extended at its base.

In Fig. 79, a 10 KW triphase motor M, is shown, connected to a hoist. Here F, is the field winding, and A, the winding on the rotating armature.

A marked advantage possessed by multiphase motors, either of the diphase or triphase type, lies in their simplicity. They require no commutator, and their winding is of a very simple description. They are compact and require the minimum amount of attention. These facts, taken in connection with the facility of transforming alternating-current pressures, have given a great impetus to the manufacture and use of multiphase motors.

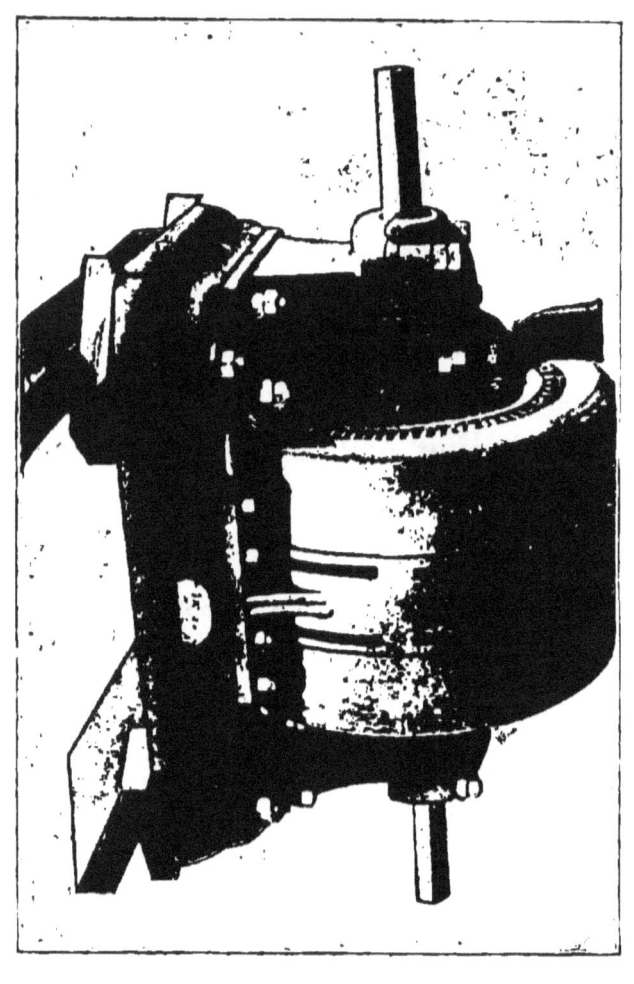

FIG. 80.—TRIPHASE MOTOR. FOR USE ON CEILINGS OR ELEVATOR BEAMS.

Fig. 80 shows a form of triphase motor suitable for driving line shafting. It is secured in an inverted position to a ceiling or elevated beam.

The multiphase motor is sometimes used as a starter for a large uniphase synchronous motor. Fig. 81 represents such an arrangement. Here the diphase motor M, is capable of being moved forward on its base by the wheel H, so that its pulley Q, engages by friction with the pulley R, of the large synchronous motor S. This is done in order to bring the large synchronous motor up to, or slightly in excess of, its synchronizing speed. As soon as this speed has been attained, the circuit of the uniphase motor is closed, enabling it to be operated from that circuit and to absorb energy from the generator at the transmitting end of the line. The friction clutch C,

FIG. 81.—UNIPHASE SYNCHRONOUS MOTOR WITH MULTIPHASE STARTING MOTOR.

is then operated to connect the pulley P, and its load with the synchronous motor, which torque can now be taken by the motor without its falling out of synchronism. The diphase motor M, is then withdrawn and stopped.

CHAPTER XI.

ALTERNATING-CURRENT TRANSMISSIONS.

As we have already pointed out, economy in electric transmission necessitates the use of high pressure in the line when the distance between generating and receiving station is great, and that considerable practical difficulty exists in obtaining continuous-current translating devices which may be operated by it.

The use of alternating currents for the transmission of power obviates the difficulty as regards high-pressure translating devices, since by means of the alternating-current transformer, the high pressure on the line can readily be transformed at the generator and motor to any desired low pressure.

Alternating-current systems of transmission may be classified as uniphase or multiphase. The use of any uniphase power system is open, however, to the objection that, as yet, no electric motor of any considerable size has been designed, which will start from rest when directly connected with such circuit. For this reason the tendency of recent engineering practice has been towards multiphase transmission systems.

In order to compare the relative advantages of economy between uniphase and multiphase systems, so far as relates to the weight of the conductors employed, some common criterion must be adopted as a basis of comparison. It is obvious, if a given weight of copper be employed in a uniphase system of transmission, at a pressure of say 4,000 volts, that it would be possible to reduce this weight of copper either on a uniphase or a multiphase system by employing a higher pressure. Consequently, the basis of comparison must be a given maximum effective pressure. This maximum permissible pressure might be measured between any wire in the system and the ground, or, between any pair of conductors independently of the ground. The latter is usually the basis of comparison, since, when circuit wires are buried side by side in a conduit, or are suspended side by side from poles, it is the insulation between these wires which determines the electric security of the system and this insulation is not from a practical standpoint to be regarded as the mere number of ohms, or megohms, existing between the conductors, but in their latent capability of maintaining this degree of insulation under all normal circumstances.

Let us suppose that the maximum permissible pressure between any pair of wires

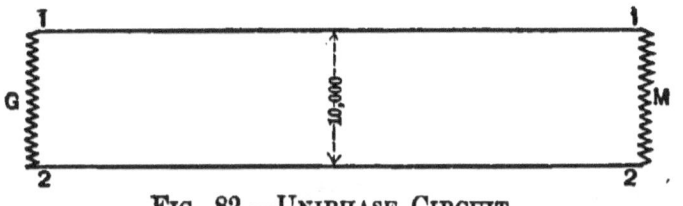

FIG. 82.—UNIPHASE CIRCUIT.

is fixed at 10,000 volts effective, as indicated by a voltmeter connected between them; then the uniphase system would have 10,000 volts between its single pair of wires, as shown in Fig. 82, where G, is the generator, M, the motor and 1 1 and 2 2, the wires. A four-wire diphase system would have 10,000 volts between the wires of each circuit, as shown in Fig. 83. The three-wire diphase system would have 10,000 volts between the outside wires and 7,070

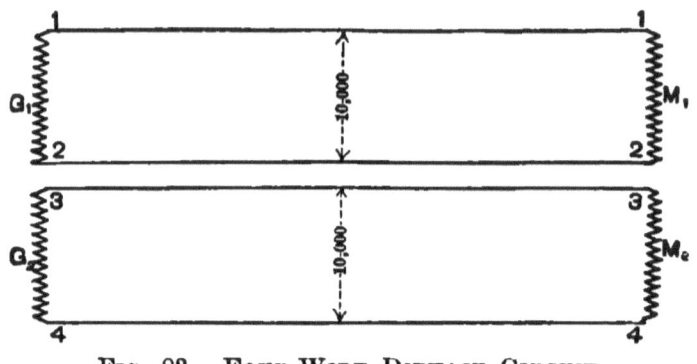

FIG. 83.—FOUR-WIRE DIPHASE CIRCUIT.

volts between neighboring wires, as shown in Fig. 84, and a triphase system would

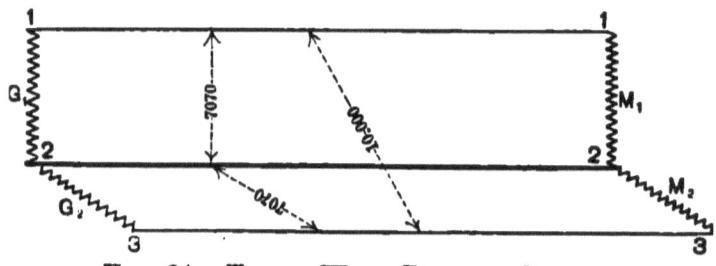

FIG. 84.—THREE-WIRE DIPHASE SYSTEM.

have 10,000 volts between any two of the three wires, as shown in Fig. 85. Under these conditions the uniphase, and the *independent-circuit diphase* or, the *four-wire diphase*, possess the same relative economy in conductors. The triphase system, however, requires 25 per cent. less copper, altogether, than either the uniphase, or the

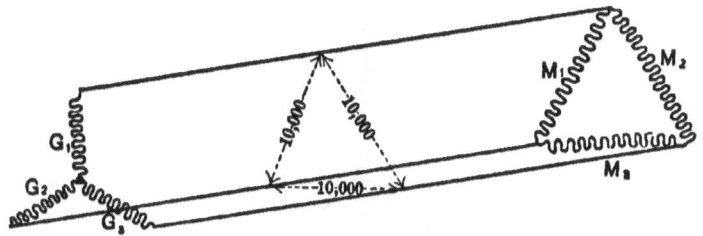

FIG. 85.—TRIPHASE SYSTEM.

independent-circuit diphase, while the *interlinked*, or *three-wire diphase*, requires 45 per cent. more copper than the uniphase, on the basis of Fig. 84, since when the maximum effective pressure is reached between wires 1 and 3, the working pressure is only 7,070 volts. If the pressure between outside conductors could be neglected, and

10,000 volts retained between working wires, then the three-wire diphase would save 27 per cent. in copper over either the uniphase, or the four-wire diphase, and

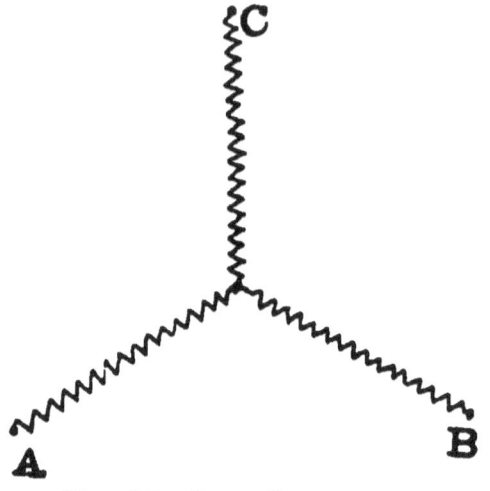

Fig. 86.—Star Connection.

thus slightly exceed the triphase system in economy.

There are two methods of connecting the circuits of a triphase system; namely, the *star method*, and the *triangle method*.

These are illustrated in Figs. 86 and 87, respectively. Both methods have been used. The E. M. Fs. in each branch differ in phase by 1/3rd cycle, in each case.

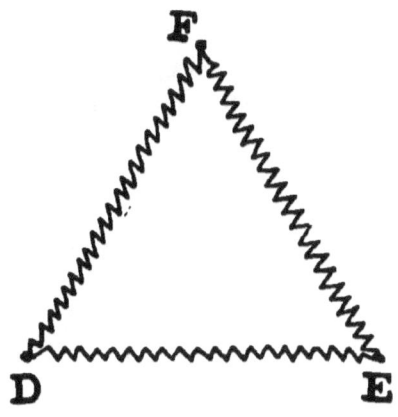

FIG. 87.—TRIANGLE OR DELTA CONNECTION.

The connections employed for step-up and step-down transformers, at each end of a transmission line, are outlined in Figs. 88 and 89, where Fig. 88 indicates a uniphase and Fig. 89 the triphase system. Here the pressure generated by the alternator and motor may be, say 1,000 volts, while that on the line may be 10,000 volts. Ob-

Fig. 88.—Step-Up and Step-Down Transformers with Uniphase System.

viously, however, the pressure between the line terminals, at the step-up transformer,

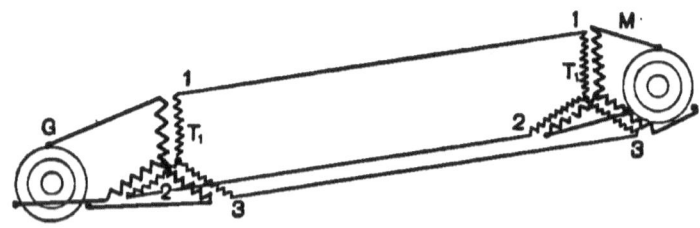

Fig. 89.—Step-Up and Step-Down Transformers of Triphase Transmission System.

will be greater than the pressure at the line terminals at the receiving end, owing to the drop in the line.

THE TRANSMISSION OF POWER. 311

No better illustration can be given of methods of alternating-current power transmission than that afforded by the system now in operation at Niagara Falls. Here energy, taken by turbines from water falling through a vertical shaft, is delivered to alternating-current circuits for transmission.

In the case of a powerful stream like Niagara, since it would be impossible to set a wheel at the foot of the falls, turbines are placed at the bottom of a pit 178 feet deep, situated a mile and a half up the river. The water that falls through the penstocks is discharged through a tunnel at the foot of the falls. The total available capacity of the tunnel is about 100,000 horse-power.

The capacity of each turbine is 5,000

Fig. 90.—Bird's-Eye View of Niagara Falls, N. Y., Showing the Electric Power-House, Wheel Pit, Subway and Tunnel in Section.

horse-power at the generator terminals. Consequently, it would be necessary to install 20 turbines in all in order to utilize the full capacity of the tunnel. Fig. 90 gives a bird's-eye view of the arrangement with the wheel pit and tunnel in section. Fig. 91, shows the short canal leading in from the river, and feeding the various wheels through their separate penstocks. $P\ P\ P$, is the penstock, or vertical iron feed water pipe through which the water falls on to the turbine. T, is the turbine, $R\ R$, the *tail race*, that is a large exit pipe through which the water passes to the tunnel after leaving the turbine. The tunnel is 7,250 feet long, 14 to 18 feet wide, and 21 feet in height, its gradient being about 1 in 150. Since a part of the tunnel passes under the city of Niagara it was necessary to prevent all possibility of eroding the walls. In order to effect this,

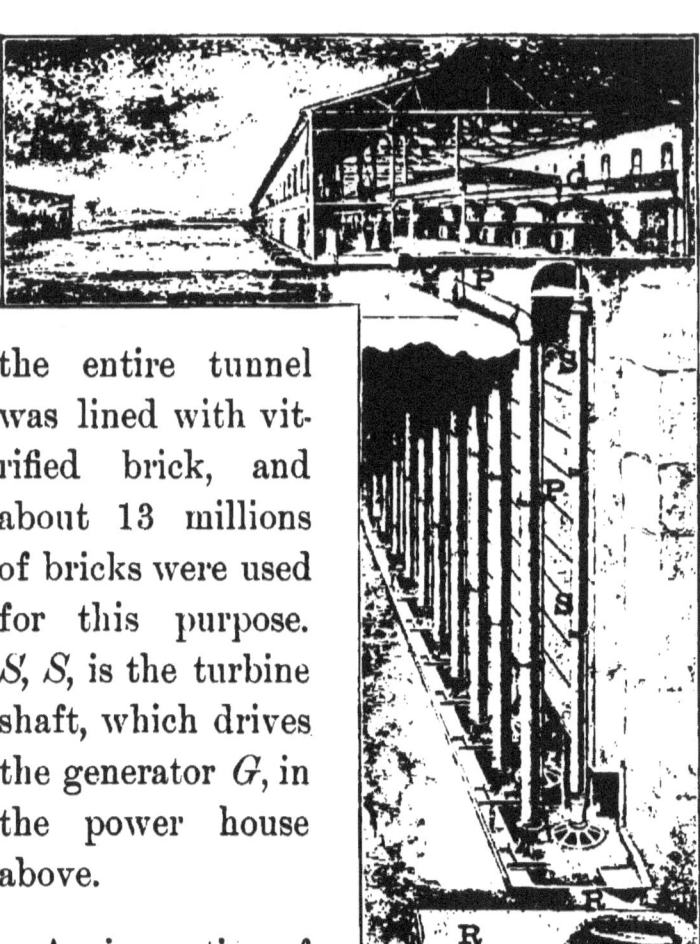

the entire tunnel was lined with vitrified brick, and about 13 millions of bricks were used for this purpose. S, S, is the turbine shaft, which drives the generator G, in the power house above.

An inspection of Fig. 92 will show in greater detail

Fig. 91.—Wheel Pit.

the manner in which the lower end of the penstock delivers its water to the turbine wheel. After falling through

FIG. 92.—ONE OF THE NIAGARA POWER COMPANY'S 5,000 HP. TURBINES DESIGNED BY FAESCH & PICCARD, GENEVA, SWITZERLAND. BUILT BY THE I. P. MORRIS COMPANY, PHILADELPHIA, PA.

the vertical pipe P, P, of Fig. 91, it passes through the inclined pipe P, P, at the lower part of the penstock, entering the body of the turbine at T, and is discharged therefrom into the tail race below. The vertical axis of the shaft of the tur-

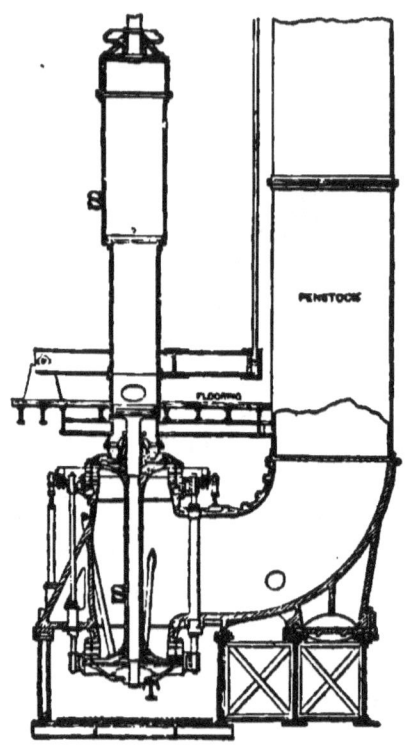

Fig. 93.—Section of the Turbine.

bine S, passes upwards to the generator, as shown more completely in Fig. 91.

A vertical section to the parts shown in Fig. 92, is given in Fig. 93, together with the upper portion of the penstock and turbine shaft. In this figure the same letters refer to the same parts.

Coming to the top of the turbine shaft, we find the generator which it drives. In this form of generator it is the field magnets which move, the armature remaining at rest. The armature is shown in Fig. 94. A, A, is the Gramme-ring diphase armature of the iron-clad type, resting upon the pedestal P, and having 187 slots cut in its surface in which the conductors are placed. There are two conductors in each slot, each conductor formed of a copper bar $1.34'' \times 0.44''$ in cross-section. The winding of the armature is in two separate circuits, so arranged that the alternating E. M. F. is generated one quarter of a wave apart in the two circuits, so that the two E. M. Fs. are in diphase relationship.

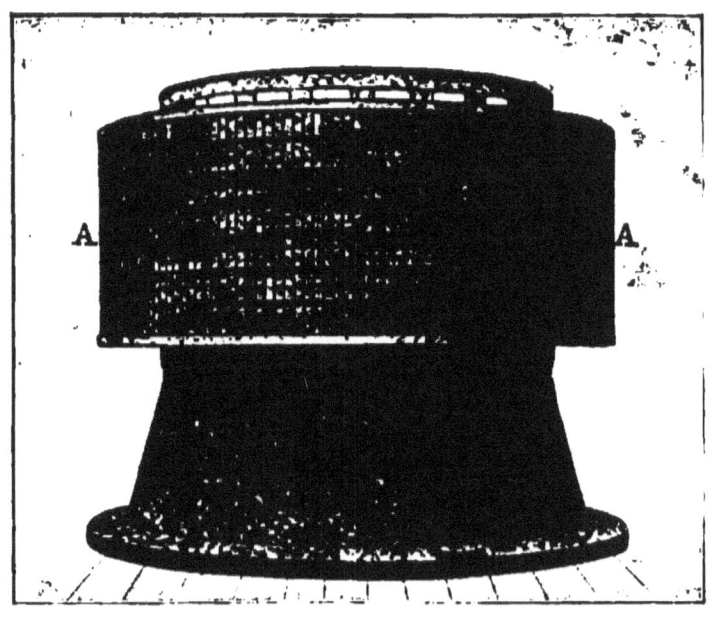

Fig. 94.—One of the 5,000 HP Armatures.

The revolving field ring, with its 12 poles, is represented separately in Fig. 95. The poles N, S, are of soft steel, rigidly bolted on the interior of the solid nickel steel ring, and the field spools are represented in position. These field coils are wound on brass spools and are all perma-

FIG. 95.—FIELD RING WITH POLES AND BOBBINS IN PLACE.

nently excited by a continuous current from a separate generator. The field ring is 11' 7" in diameter, and revolves at 250 revolutions per minute. The cover of the field ring is shown in an inverted position in Fig. 96. *A*, *A*, *A*, are ventilating apertures in the cover, intended to draw in cool air for the ventilation of the armature during rotation, while *C*, is a central aperture for the reception of the turbine shaft.

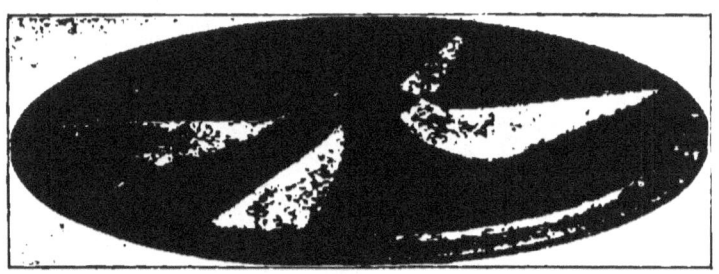

Fig. 96.—The Driver for the Field Ring.

Since the field magnets revolve around the fixed armature, it is necessary to firmly attach the field to the shaft. This is effected by means of the cover just described. A completed machine is represented in position in Fig. 97.

A vertical cross-section of the machine

through the axis of the shaft is shown in
Fig. 98. *s, s, s*, is the turbine shaft to the
top of which is firmly secured the moving

Fig. 97.—The First Generator in Position in the Power House at Niagara.

field ring *F. R.*, through the driver *D*.
The poles *p, p*, have their coils excited by
current supplied through the collector rings

322   THE ELECTRIC MOTOR AND

S. Brushes, not shown in the figure, rest on these rings, supported on the brush

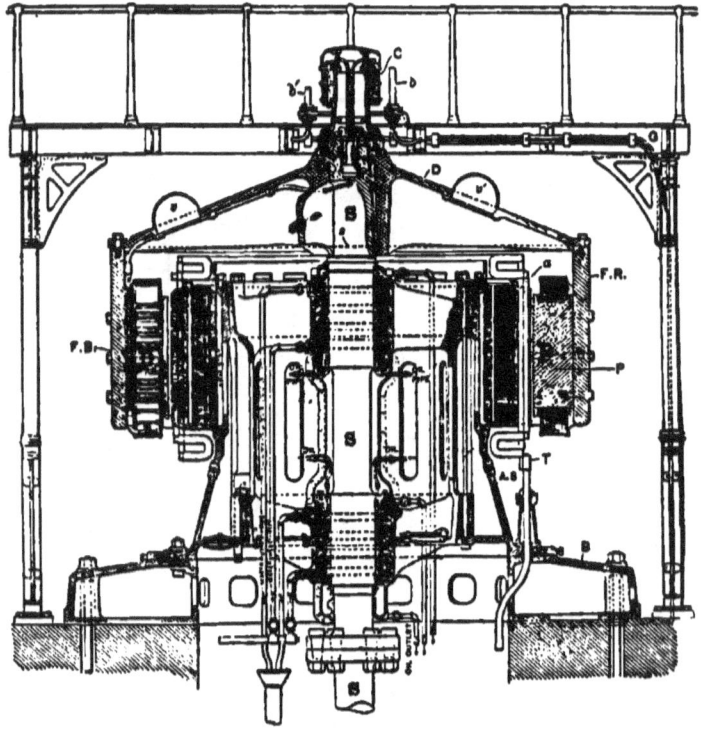

FIG. 98.—VERTICAL SECTION OF ONE OF THE 5,000 HP GENERATORS.

holder bars *b, b,* attached to the platform over the machine. The current is supplied to these brush holders through conductors G, leading to an independent generator at 175 volts pressure. a, a, is the fixed armature ring supported on the cast-iron base B.

The electric connections necessary for the local and long distance distribution of power are represented in Fig. 99, for two 5,000 horse-power generators. The pressure supplied by the alternators in each of their two separate diphase circuits is from 2,000 to 2,400 volts, according to requirements. The two generators are indicated at 1 and 2. Their four wires are led to separate switches S and S''. Each switch is arranged so that it can either be disconnected altogether, as shown in the diagram, or can make connection between the generator and either of the sets of bus-bars A and B. Thus, if the switch be thrown on one side, it will connect the four generator wires to the four bus-bar wires *A*, while

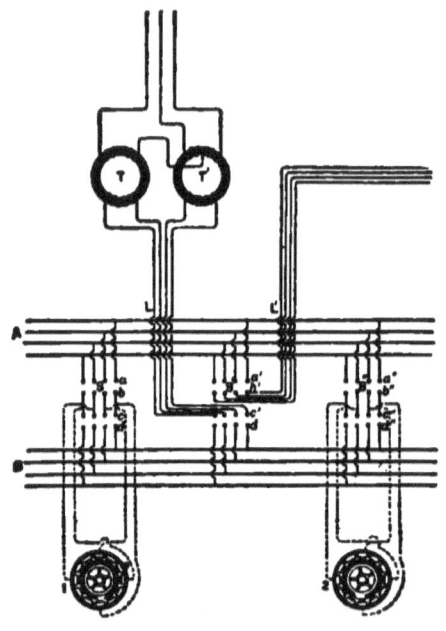

FIG. 99.—DIAGRAM SHOWING THE CONNECTIONS OF THE GENERATORS WITH LOCAL AND LONG DISTANCE FEEDERS.

if it be thrown on the other side, it will connect the generator wires to the four bus-bar wires *B*.

The two sets of bus-bars are arranged so as to enable the two separate generators to be employed independently; one, for example, to supply local distribution, and the other, to supply long distance distribution. The switch $S'' S'$, in the centre of the figure, enables connection to be made between the long distance wires L, and the bus-bars B, or the local circuit wires L, L', and the bus-bars A. For local distribution, a pressure of 2,000 volts is sufficient without the intervention of any step-up transformers; but for long distance transmission, as, for example, to Buffalo, the step-up transformers T, T', would be employed. These are so arranged, that when connected in the proper manner, having their primaries supplied by diphase currents, their secondaries will generate triphase currents. The three long-distance mains are represented on the secondary side. This

326   THE ELECTRIC MOTOR AND

FIG. 100.—THE INTERNAL CONSTRUCTION OF A LARGE STATIC TRANSFORMER. THIS TRANSFORMER REDUCES THE PRESSURE OF THE TWO-PHASE ALTERNATING CURRENT FROM 2,400 TO 200 VOLTS.

transfer from the diphase to the triphase system is introduced for the purpose of saving copper in the line transmission.

THE TRANSMISSION OF POWER. 327

FIG. 101.—1,000 HP TRANSFORMER.

Fig. 100, shows the internal parts of a large 1,000 horse-power transformer, intended for the reduction of pressure from 2,200 to 200 volts, but it would, of course, be possible to employ similar transformers for raising the pressure, the secondary windings then being altered. This transformer belongs to the type of *oil-cooled transformers*. It is set in an iron case, represented in Fig. 101, through which oil is pumped.

An excellent illustration of the capabilities of long-distance alternating-current transmission is seen in Fig. 102. Here the power station, which might be a station like that at Niagara Falls, is represented in the lower, left-hand corner, with triphasers driven by water-wheels and supplying a pressure of 2,000 volts. The pressure is raised to 10,000 volts by means of three

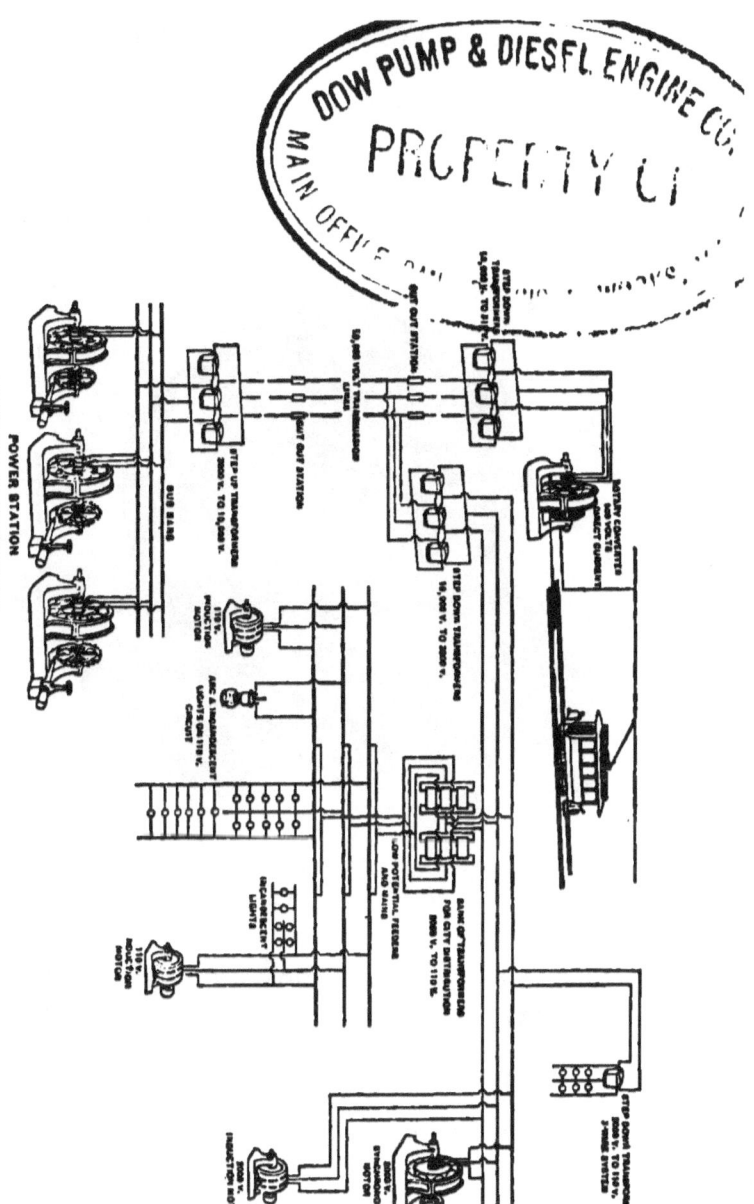

Fig. 102.—Diagram Showing an Example of Long-Distance Electric Power Transmission and Distribution.

step-up transformers, and is transmitted through the three long-distance wires to the receiving station, where it is reduced

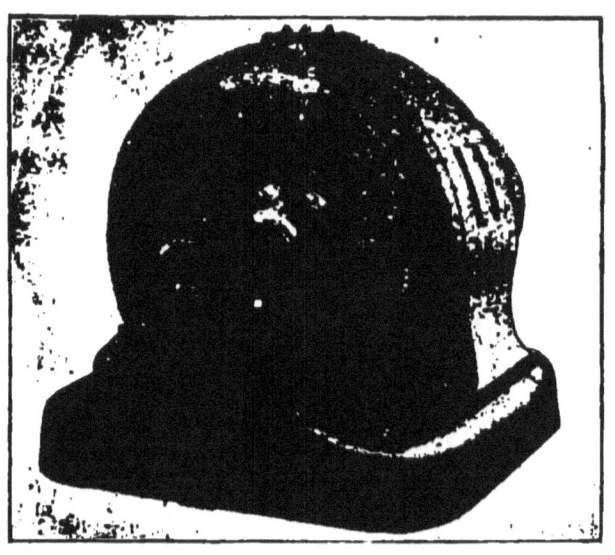

FIG. 103.—A TYPICAL ALTERNATING-CURRENT INDUCTION MOTOR OF 125 HP.

through step-down transformers to a pressure of 310 volts, in a circuit intended for street railway power transmission, and to 2,000 volts, in another circuit intended for city distribution. The 310-volt triphase-circuit is led to a *rotary converter* ; i. e., a triphase motor carrying a commutator upon which brushes rest in such a manner that as the motor armature revolves, the alternating current received at the collector rings on one side is redistributed through the commutator as a continuous current of 500 volts pressure on the other, which pressure is conveyed to the street railway mains. The 2,000-volt secondary circuits are carried through the city, and are either employed to drive triphase motors of the synchronous or non-synchronous type, or through local transformers to distribute light and power in 110-volt triphase or uniphase circuits.

A form of triphase motor of 125 horse-power, or about 94 KW, is represented in Fig. 103. Here the current is supplied through three terminals at the top of the field frame. The armature carries a collar which is so arranged that when disengaged

Fig. 104.—A 250-HP Three-Phase Alternating-Current Motor.

from its receptacle, a certain resistance is inserted in the armature circuit, but when the motor has attained full speed, the collar

THE TRANSMISSION OF POWER. 333

is thrown into its receptacle by the use of the projecting handle at the side, when this resistance is cut out of the armature circuit.

Fig. 104, represents a form of more powerful triphase motor, being adapted to supply 250 HP, or about 188 KW. Here the current is supplied through the three collector rings of the rotating portion or rotor. This produces a rotating field in the armature, under the action of which the armature attracts the field frame and is set in rotation. After the armature has reached full speed the machine acts as a synchronous motor in step with the triphase impulses received on the line.

If the motor were a uniphase machine, it would not be able to start itself from a state of rest, but once brought to full speed it would also be able to run in synchronism, although it would, probably, be more easily thrown out of step by a sudden variation of load.

The torque which a multiphase; that is, of a diphase or triphase induction motor, can exert at starting; *i. e.*, its starting torque, is often considerably greater than the torque which it will have to exert when running at full speed under full load. The starting torque of a multiphase synchronous motor is usually much less than its full load torque, but its power factor at full load is greater than that of an induction motor. This is often an advantage to the alternating-current distributing system.

CHAPTER XII.

MISCELLANEOUS APPLICATIONS OF ELECTRIC MOTORS.

ONE of the principal advantages of the electric motor is the ease with which it can be directly applied to machinery. It has been customary, in large machine shops, to employ long lines of shafting, receiving power from an engine or other prime mover, and transmitting this power to the driving pulleys of machines, either directly, or through the intervention of counter-shafts. The use of the electric motor enables each machine to be operated independently of all the others, thus avoiding the continuous expenditure of power in overcoming the friction of line shafts. Moreover, the requirements of each machine as to speed and regulation may be more readily dealt with by this means. In some cases, where machinery has to stand at an angle with the line shafting, the difficulty which would be experienced in belting to the same are entirely overcome. In other cases groups of machines may be operated each from a single motor, by the use of short lengths of counter-shaft. This is known as the *group system*.

The number of machines to which electric motive power has been applied is so great that space will prevent more than a cursory description of them. We will, therefore, select some of the more prominent of these applications, although many others will occur to the reader.

The application of the electric motor to the driving of a screw machine is shown

FIG. 105.—ELECTRIC MONITOR OR SCREW MACHINE.

in Fig. 105. Here the armature of the electric motor, mounted on the lathe head, is shown at A. A switch is provided at S, for starting the motor, which is an ordinary continuous-current machine.

Fig 106, shows the application of a continuous-current electric motor directly

FIG. 106.—ELECTRIC PIPE CUTTING MACHINE.

coupled to a pipe cutting machine. Fig. 107, shows the application of a continuous-current electric motor, to a punch press.

Here the motor is geared to the shaft of the machine.

The electric motor is particularly adapted for driving such machinery as is used at irregular intervals, and where but little power is required. Of course, under these circumstances, it would not be economical to install a steam engine and boiler. An instance of this kind is found in the driving of the bellows of church organs. Water motors, formerly employed for this purpose, have been largely superseded by electric motors. An electric motor attached to a house or church organ is represented in Fig. 108. M, is a small continuous-current motor, belted to the pulley of the bellows mechanism. A regulator R, is so arranged, that if the rate of pumping is not sufficient to maintain the full wind pressure, a resistance will be cut out of the circuit and the motor will be accelerated. The starting box S, is placed by the side

Fig. 107.—Electric Punch Press with Dividing Head or Index.

of the keyboard, so as to permit the organist readily to start and stop the motor at will.

THE TRANSMISSION OF POWER. 341

Fig. 108.—Electric Motor Applied to Organ Bellows.

The application of the electric motor to the pumping of water is shown in Fig. 109. Here a continuous-current motor M,

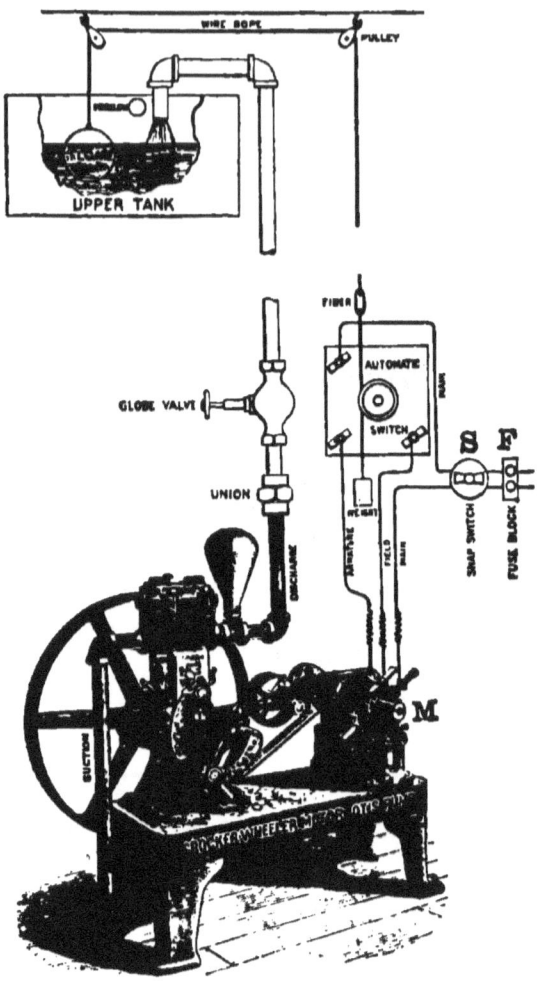

Fig. 109.—Electric Motor Applied to Pumping in Dwelling House.

operated from incandescent electric light mains, is belted to the pump pulley. The supply wires to the motor are led through a fuse block *F*, to the double-pole snap switch *S*, from which they proceed to an automatic switch. This latter is provided for the stopping and starting of the motor, under the control of a ball float in a water tank. When the water in the tank reaches a certain height, the rising of the ball lowers the weight and suddenly opens the armature circuit. On the contrary, when the water in the tank falls too low, the descent of the float raises the weight, and starts the motor slowly. In all such cases, where motors are installed under conditions where they are likely to run for weeks without attention, it is advisable to employ motors of as slow a speed and substantial a construction as possible, so as to diminish the wear and tear, and hence the attention required. It is, for this reason, even advisable to employ a motor of more than sufficient size to do the work required, since under these circumstances it will run with very little effort.

The motors, above illustrated, have been all of the continuous-current type. It is needless to say, however, that alternating-current motors could be employed in their stead, provided that they are of the multiphase type, so as to permit them to start from rest.

Fig. 110 shows a Gatling gun, in which an electric motor is employed for the purpose of operating the breech mechanism. The certainty and precision with which the motor will introduce and release the cartridges, renders this application of the electric motor very advantageous.

THE TRANSMISSION OF POWER.   345

The applications of the diamond drill for prospecting in mining districts are well known. The electric motor provides an

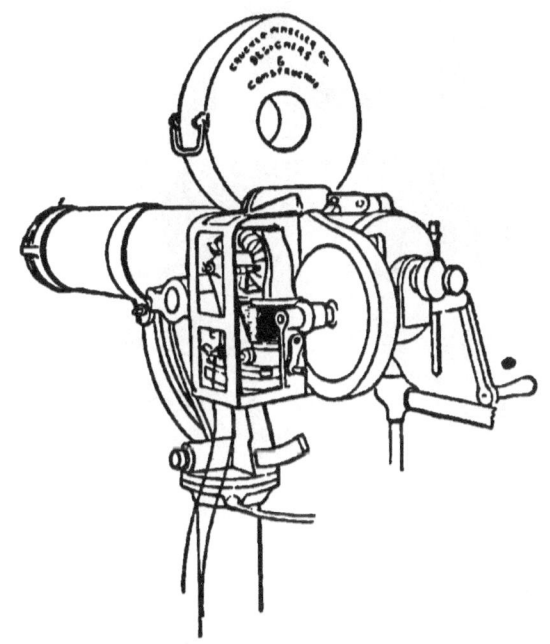

FIG. 110.—GATLING GUN. OPERATED BY ELECTRIC MOTOR.

exceedingly convenient means for driving such drills, when electric power is available. Their use in mining districts has come into favor, owing to the fact that the solid core of the rock mined is brought out by this drill. Fig. 111, shows a form

FIG. 111.—ELECTRIC DIAMOND PROSPECTING DRILL.

of this machine with a continuous-current electric motor applied to drive it.

Electric motors are often applied both

to elevators in buildings, and to hoists in mines. In the latter case, the ease with

FIG. 112.—THOMSON-HOUSTON PORTABLE ELECTRIC HOIST. BAND CLUTCH TYPE.

which the power can be carried to different parts of the mine renders the electric driving of such hoists very advantageous. An illustration of a continuous-current motor, connected with a portable electric hoist, is

Fig. 113.—An Alternating-Current Induction Motor Geared to a Hoist.

shown in Fig. 112. A similar form of hoist driven by an alternating-current induction motor is shown in Fig. 113.

In the commercial sale of electric power, whether for lighting or for motive purposes, a necessity exists for carefully

FIG. 114.—1/8 HP ELECTRIC FAN. WITH WIRE GUARD AND SWITCH FOR RUNNING FAST OR SLOW.

measuring the amount of supply to each consumer. For this purpose a variety of electric meters are employed. The electric meters commonly in use employ a small motor driven by the electric power, at a speed proportionate to the rate of supply.

Probably there is no purpose for which small powers are more required during

Fig. 115.—Fan Motor.

certain seasons of the year, than for driving rotary fans. A great variety of forms have been devised, varying not only with the character of the fan, but also with the position in which it is located. Fan motors are made to operate, both on continuous and on alternating-current circuits. For

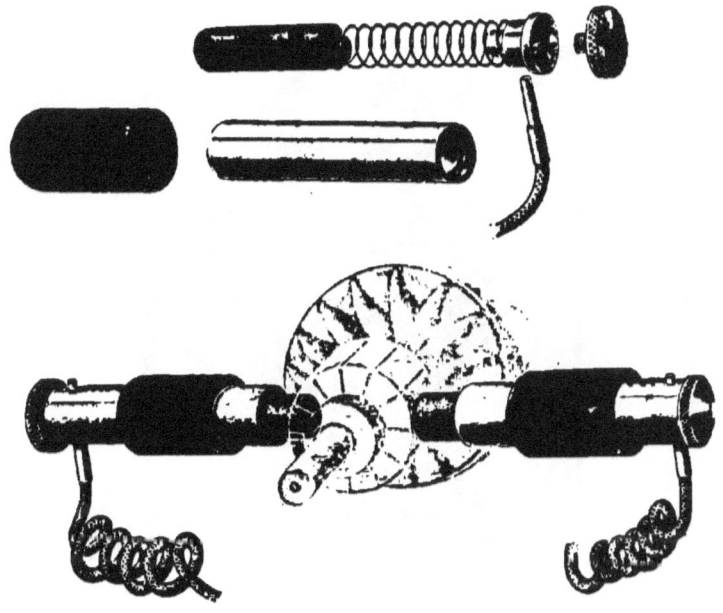

Fig. 116.—Fan Motor Brushes in Detail.

such small alternating-current motors multiphase circuits are not required. A fan motor always starts with no load, be-

352   THE ELECTRIC MOTOR AND

yond the friction of its own bearings, but the load increases rapidly as the speed increases, the activity developed being, approximately, as the cube of the

FIG. 117.—No. 3 FAN MOTOR.

velocity. The fan is generally attached directly to the motor shaft. Fig. 114 is an illustration of a continuous-current fan motor, arranged for various speeds. Here,

THE TRANSMISSION OF POWER. 353

as is usual where the motor is in a position in which it may be touched, it is provided with a wire guard.

FIG. 118.—No. 1 FAN OUTFIT FOR ARC CIRCUITS (CONSTANT CURRENTS).

The motor described in Fig. 114 is exposed to view. Frequently, however, the motor is inclosed in a cast-iron case, as shown in Fig. 115. In such cases special attention has to be paid to the brushes and commutator, since they run out of view. Fig. 116, shows the details of a form of

FIG. 119.—CEILING FAN AND MOTOR.

brush employed in the motor of Fig. 115. Here, it will be seen that carbon cylindrical brushes are employed which are maintained in pressure upon the commutator by the action of a spiral spring.

Fig. 117, shows an alternating-current

Fig. 120.—No. 2 (1/4 HP) Fan Outfit, Set up as an Exhaust.

fan motor, also enclosed. Fig. 118, shows a form of fan motor intended to be operated on a series-arc circuit. Since the pressure employed on such a circuit is generally high, this motor requires to be carefully insulated.

For the cooling of rooms, the fans are

FIG. 121.—DIRECT-CONNECTED EXHAUST FANS AND LUNDELL MOTORS.

sometimes suspended from the ceilings. In this case the fan blades are driven in a horizontal plane by a suitably supported motor. Fig. 119, shows a form of ceiling

THE TRANSMISSION OF POWER. 357

Fig. 122.—Electric Capstans.

fan motor, adapted for continuous-current circuits. Here the motor is placed below the fan blades.

The electric motor is frequently used for ventilating purposes. In Fig. 120 a motor, is shown in position for driving an exhaust fan. Another form of such motor is shown in Fig. 121.

Fig. 122 shows the application of the electric motor for driving a capstan on board ship. In this particular case the motor is operated on a 110-volt continuous-current circuit, and has a capacity of about 5 KW.

INDEX.

A

Active Conductor, Circular Flux of, 84, 85.
Activity, 11.
——— of Electric Circuit, 53, 54, 55.
——— of Motor, 157, 158.
———, Thermal, 55.
———, Unit of, 11, 12.
———, Wasted, 55.
Alternating-Current Dynamo, 257, 258.
——— Current Motors, 241 to 283.
——— Current Transformers, 247.
——— Current Transmission, 302 to 334.
——— E. M. F., 242.
Alternator, 257, 258.
———, Collector Rings of, 258.
———, Monocyclic, 275, 276.
Ampere, 35.

Ampere Turns, 131.
Analogue of Electric Flow, 67 to 70.
Armature Core of Motor, 162.
———, Monocyclic, 273.
——— of Motor, 110.
———, Smooth-Core, 174, 175.
———, Smooth-Core, Completed, 179, 180.
———, Toothed-Core, 174, 175.
———, Toothed-Core, Completed, 180.
Armatures, Disc, 171, 172, 173.
———, Drum, 170.
———, 5,000 Horse-Power, 318.
———, Ring, 170.
Automatic Self-Oiling Bearings, 189, 190.

B

Babbitt Metal, 188.
Back Pressure, Electric, 49.
Barlow, 94.
——— Wheel Motor, 95.
Bar-Magnet, Flux of, 79.
Battery, Voltaic, 37.
———, Voltaic, Series-Connected, 38.
Bearings, Automatic Self-Oiling, 189, 190.
———, Self-Oiling, 163.

INDEX.   361

Belt Tightener, 200.
Bluestone Voltaic Cell, 36.
Board of Trade Unit, 160.
Boiler and Steam Engine, Low Efficiency of, 26 to 28.
Box, Cut-Out, 208.
Broken Circuit, 32.
Brushes, Adjustment of, 211.
———, Arrangement of, 186.
Brush Holders, 187.

C

C. E. M. F., 49.
Cell, Bluestone Voltaic, 36.
Choking Effect, 245.
Circuit, Broken, 32.
———, Closed, 32.
———, Completed, 32.
———, Driven, 248.
———, Driving, 248.
———, Electric, 31, 32.
———, Electric, Activity of, 53, 54, 55.
———, Made, 32.
———, Open, 32.
———, Primary, 248.

362   INDEX.

Circuit, Resistance of, 34.
———, Secondary, 248.
———, Uniphase, 305.
Circular Flux of Active Conductor, 84, 85.
——— Mil, 42.
——— Mil-Foot, 42.
Closed Circuit, 32.
Commutation, Diameter of, 164.
———, Sparkless, 212.
Commutator, Two-Part, 184.
Completed Circuit, 32.
Compound-Wound Motor, 156, 157.
Connections of Shunt-Wound Motor, 207, 208.
Conservation of Energy, Doctrine of, 2.
Constant-Potential Mains, 147.
Continuous-Current Motor, Forms of, 164 to 169.
——— E. M. F., 242.
Convertor, Rotary, 331.
Core of Motor Armature, 162.
Cores, Laminated, of Motors, 176.
Coulomb, 44.
——— per-Second, 44.
Counter Electromotive Force, 49, 59, 60.
Current, Alternating, 242.
———, Electric, 30.
——— Strength, 34.
——— Strength or Flow, Unit of, 35.

Currents, Eddy, 175, 176, 215, 216.
———, Stray, 215, 216.
Cut-Out Box, 208.
Cycle, 242.

D

Davenport, 104.
Density, Magnetic, Unit of, 134.
Diagrams of Torque, 123, 124.
Diameter of Commutation, 164.
Diphase Field, 292.
——— Field-Frame, 292.
———, Four-Conductor, Diagram of System, 264, 265.
——— Four-Wire Circuit, 306.
———, Independent Circuit, 307.
——— Motor, 283.
———, Three-Conductor System, 266, 267.
——— Three-Wire System, 306.
——— System, 263.
——— System, Connections of, 282.
Disc Armatures, 171, 172, 173.
——— Dynamo, Faraday's, 98 to 101.
Double-Pole Switch, 208.
Driven Circuit, 248.
Driving Circuit, 248.

Drop or Fall, 52.
Drum Armatures, 170.
Dynamo, Alternating-Current, 257, 258.
——— Electric Machine, 36, 37.

E

E. M. F., 33.
———, Continuous, 242.
———, Effective, 144.
Early Faraday Motor, 88, 89.
Eddy Currents, 175, 176, 215, 216.
Effect, Choking, 245.
Effective E. M. F., 144.
——— Resistance, 245.
Efficiencies of Motors, 159, 213.
Efficiency of Machine, 24, 25.
Electric and Hydraulic Resistance, Analogy Between, 39, 40.
——— Back Pressure, 49.
——— Circuit, 31, 32.
——— Current, 30.
——— Flow, 30.
——— Motor, Advantages of, 217, 218.
——— Motors, Miscellaneous Applications of, 335 to 358.

INDEX. 395

Electric Pressure, 34.
——— Sources, 30.
——— Transmission, Commercial and Electric Conditions of Problem, 223 to 240.
——— Transmission of Power, 217 to 241.
Electro-Dynamic Force, 97, 120, 121, 122.
Electromagnetic Rotation, 76.
Electromotive Force, 33.
——— Force, Counter, 49.
——— Force, Unit of, 35.
Elias' Motor, 108, 109.
Energy, Definition of, 3.
———, Doctrine of Conservation of, 2.
———, Hysteretic Loss of, 214.
———, Indestructibility of, 2.
——— of Food, Transference of, 8.
———, Rate-of-Expending, 11.
———, Sources of, 19 to 28.
Entrefer, 182.
Ether Streams, 81.
———, Universal, 80, 81.

F

Factor, Power, 254.
Fan Motors, 349 to 356.

INDEX.

Faraday, 74.
—— Motor, Early, 88, 89.
Faraday's Disc, 98 to 101.
Field, Magnetic, 77.
—— Magnetic, of Motor, 110.
—— Rheostat, of Motor, 210.
——, Triphase Rotating, 290, 291.
Fields, Diphase, 292.
Five-Thousand Horse-Power Armature, 318.
Flow, Electric, 30.
——, Electric, Analogue of, 67 to 70.
Flux, Leakage, 136.
——, Magnetic, 77.
——, Magnetic, Unit of, 131.
——, Stray, of Motor, 136.
Food, Transference of Energy of, 8.
Foot-Pound, 9.
Foot-Pound-per-Second, 12.
Force, Electro-Dynamic, 97, 120, 121, 122.
——, Electromotive, 33.
——, Magnetomotive, 130.
Forward Lead of Motor Brushes, 212.
Four-Wire Diphase Circuit, 306, 307.
Frequency, 243.
Froment's Motor, 114, 115.
Fuse, Safety, 208.

G

Gauss, 134.
Gilbert, 131.

H

Holders, Brush, 187.
Horse-Power, 12.
Hydraulic Flow, Gradient of Water Pressure During, 61, 62.
——— Transmission, 15.
Hysteresis, 214.
———, Magnetic, 214.

I

Impedance, 247.
Independent Circuit, Diphase, 307.
Indestructibility of Energy, 2.
Induction Motor, 279.
——— Motors, 289.
——— Multiphase Motors, 289.
Installation and Operation of Motors, 200 to 216.
——— of Shunt-Wound Motor, 205, 206.
Intake of Machine, 22.
Inter-Linked Diphase, 307.
International Unit of Work, 9.

J

Jacoby's Electric Motor, 101 to 104.
Joule, Definition of, 9, 10.
Joule-per-Second, 12, 48.

L

Laminated Cores of Motors, 176.
Law, Ohm's, 35.
Lead, Forward, of Motor Brushes, 212.
Leads, 52.
Leakage Flux, 136.
———, Magnetic, 136.

M

M. M. F., 131.
Machine, Dynamo-Electric, 36, 37.
———, Efficiency of, 24.
———, In-Take of, 22.
———, Multipolar, 113.
———, Output of, 23.
———, Sextipolar, 113.
Made Circuit, 2.

INDEX. 369

Magnetic Circuit of Motor, 28 to 130.
——— Field, 77.
——— Flux, 77.
——— Hysteresis, 214.
——— Leakage, 136.
——— Resistance, Unit of, 132.
——— Saturation, 134.
Magnetism, Rotary, 292.
Magnetomotive Force, 130.
——— Force, Units of, 131.
Mains, Constant-Potential, 147.
Microhms, 41.
Mil, 42.
Miscellaneous Applications of the Electric Motor, 335 to 358.
Monocyclic Alternator, 275, 276.
——— Armature, 273.
——— Armature Winding, 273.
——— System, 270 to 279.
——— System, Diagram of Distribution by, 277, 278.
Motor, Activity of, 157, 158.
——— Armature, Core of, 162.
———, Armature of, 110.
——— Brushes, Adjustment of, 211.
———, Circumstances Affecting Speed of, 140 to 143.

Motor, Circumstances Affecting Torque of, 138, 139.
———, Classification of Losses of Energy in, 213.
———, Compound-Wound, 156, 157.
———, Electric, Advantages of, 217, 218.
———, Elementary Theory of, 119 to 161.
———, Froment's, 114, 115.
———, Induction, 279.
———, Magnetic Circuit of, 128.
———, Magnetic Field of, 110.
———, Multiphase Induction, 294, 295.
———, Quadripolar, 197.
———, Separately-Excited, 111.
———, Series-Wound, 154, 155.
———, Shunt-Wound, 152, 153.
Motors, Alternating-Current, 242.
———, Efficiency of, 159, 160, 213.
———, Fan, 349 to 356.
———, Induction, 289.
———, Installation and Operation of, 200 to 216.
———, Synchronous Multiphase, 289.
Multiphase Alternating-Current System, 263.
——— Induction Motors, 289, 294, 295.
——— Synchronous Motors, 289.
Multipolar Machine, 113.

N

Negative Pole of Source, 31.
Niagara Transmission, 311 to 334.

O

Oersted, 90, 91, 132.
Oersted's Magnetic Experiments, 90 to 93.
Ohm, 35.
Ohm's Law, 35.
Oil-Cooled Transformer, 328.
Open Circuit, 32.
Operation and Installation of Motors, 200 to 216.
Output of Machine, 23.

P

Pacinotti, 115.
Pacinotti's Motor, 116 to 118.
Phase, Displacement of, 256.
Pneumatic Transmission, 15.
Pole, Negative, of Source, 31.
————, Positive, of Source, 31.
Positive Pole of Source, 31.
Power, Electric Transmission of, 217, 241.

Power Factor, 254.
——— Houses, 220.
Pressure, Back, Electric, 49.
———, Drop or Fall of, 52.
———, Electric, 34.
Primary Circuit, 248.

Q

Quadripolar Motors, 197, 198, 199.
Quantity, Electric, Unit of, 44.

R

Reactance, 243.
Reluctance, 132.
———, Specific, 135.
Reluctivity, 135.
Resistance, Electric, Unit of, 35.
——— of Circuit, 34.
———, Specific, 40.
———, Total Effective, 245.
———, Unit of, 35.
Resisting Torque, 143.
Resistivity, 40.
———, Effect of Temperature on, 43.

Rheostat, Field, of Motor, 210.
———, Starting, 202, 203, 204.
Ring Armatures, 170.
Ritchie, 105.
Ritchie's Motor, 106, 107.
River, Energy of, 6.
Rope Transmission, 15.
Rotary Converter, 331.
——— Magnetism, 292.
Rotating Field, Triphase, 290, 291.
——— Magnetic Field, 284 to 301.
——— Magnetic Field, Diagram of, 285.
Rotation, Electromagnetic, 76.
Rotor, Definition of, 110.

S

Safety Fuse, 208.
Saturation, Magnetic, 134.
Secondary Circuit, 248.
Separately-Excited Motor, 111.
Series-Connected Voltaic Battery, 38.
Series Connection, 37, 38.
Series-Wound Motor, 154, 155.
Sextipolar Machine, 113.
Shunt-Wound Motor, 152, 153.

374 INDEX.

Shunt-Wound Motor, Connections of, 207, 208.
——, Installation of, 205, 206.
Smooth-Core Armature, 174, 175.
Solar Energy, Varieties of, 21, 22.
Sources, Electric, 30.
—— of Energy, 19 to 28.
—— of Energy, Classification of, 19.
Sparkless Commutation, 212.
Specific Reluctance, 135.
—— Resistance, 40.
Speed of Motor, Circumstances Affecting, 140 to 143.
Star Connection of Triphaser, 308.
Starting Rheostat, 202, 203, 204.
Stator, Definition of, 110.
Steam Engine and Boiler, Efficiency of, 26 to 28.
Step-Down Transformers, 250.
Step-Up Transformers, 251.
Stray Currents, 215, 216.
—— Flux of Motor, 136.
Stream Lines, 81.
Strength of Current, 34.
Structure and Classification of Motors, 162 to 199.
Sturgeon, 96.
Switch, Double-Pole, 208.
Synchronous Multiphase Motors, 289.

INDEX.

System, Diphase, 263.
———, Monocyclic, 270 to 279.
———, Multiphase Alternating-Current, 263.
———, Triphase, 263, 264.

T

Temperature, Effect of, on Resistivity of Metals, 43.
Theory, Elementary, of Motor, 119, 120.
Thermal Activity, 55.
Three-Wire Diphase, 307.
Toothed-Core Armature, 174, 175.
Torque, Definition of, 122.
———, Diagrams of, 123, 124.
——— of Motor, Circumstances Affecting, 138, 139.
———, Resisting, 143.
Total Effective Resistance, 245.
Transformer, Alternating-Current, 247.
———, Oil-Cooled, 228.
Transformers, 247.
———, Step-Down, 250.
———, Step-Up, 251.
Transmission, Alternating-Current, 302 to 334.
———, Hydraulic, 15.

Transmission of Power, Electric, 217, 241.
———, Pneumatic, 15.
———, Rope, 15.
———, Systems of, 14.
Triangle Connection of Triphaser, 308.
Triphase Alternator, 269, 270.
——— Motor, 297 to 299.
———, Three-Wire System, 268.
———, Six-Wire System, 267.
——— System, 263, 264, 306.
——— System, Connections of, 281.
Triphaser, 267.
Two-Part Commutator, 184.
Typical Electric Transmission System, 219, 220.

U

Uniphase Circuit, 305.
Unit, International, of Work, 9.
——— of Activity, 11, 12.
——— of Current Strength or Flow, 35.
——— of Electric Activity, 48.
——— of Electric Quantity, 44.
——— of Electric Work, 247.
——— of Electromotive Force, 35.
——— of Magnetic Density, 134.
——— of Magnetic Resistance, 132.

Unit of Resistance, 35.
Units of Magnetic Flux, 131.
——— of Magnetomotive Force, 131.
——— of Work, 9.
Universal Ether, 80, 81.

V

Varieties of Solar Energy, 21, 22.
Vertical Section of 5,000 Horse-Power Generator, 322.
Voltage, 37.
Volt, 35.
Voltaic Battery, 37.
Volt-Coulomb, 47.

W

Wasted Activity, 35.
Watermotive Force, 60, 61.
Watt, 12, 48.
Weber, 131.
Winding, Teaser, of Monocycler, 272.
Work, International Unit of, 9.
———, Rate-of-Doing, 11.
———, Units of, 9.

Elementary Electro-Technical Series.

BY
EDWIN J. HOUSTON, Ph.D. and A. E. KENNELLY, D.Sc.

Alternating Electric Currents,
Electric Heating,
Electromagnetism,
Electricity in Electro-Therapeutics,
Electric Arc Lighting,
Electric Incandescent Lighting,
Electric Motors,
Electric Street Railways,
Electric Telephony,
Electric Telegraphy.

Cloth, profusely illustrated.   *Price, $1.00 per volume.*

The above volumes have been prepared to satisfy a demand which exists on the part of the general public for reliable information relating to the various branches of electro-technics. In them will be found concise and authoritative information concerning the several departments of electrical science treated, and the reputation of the authors, and their recognized ability as writers, are a sufficient guarantee as to the accuracy and reliability of the statements. The entire issue, although published in a series of ten volumes, is, nevertheless so prepared that each volume is complete in itself, and can be understood independently of the others. The books are well printed on paper of special quality, profusely illustrated, and handsomely bound in covers of a special design.

Copies of these or any other electrical books published will be sent by mail, POSTAGE PREPAID, *to any address in the world, on receipt of price.*

The W. J. Johnston Company, Publishers,
253 BROADWAY, NEW YORK.

THIRD EDITION. GREATLY ENLARGED

A DICTIONARY OF

Electrical Words, Terms, and Phrases.

By EDWIN J. HOUSTON, Ph.D. (Princeton).

AUTHOR OF

"Advanced Primers of Electricity"; "Electricity One Hundred Years Ago and To-day," etc., etc.

Cloth, 667 large octavo pages, 582 illustrations, Price, $5.00.

Some idea of the scope of this important work and of the immense amount of labor involved in it, may be formed when it is stated that it contains definitions of about 6000 distinct words, terms, or phrases. The dictionary is not a mere word-book; the words, terms, and phrases are invariably followed by a short, concise definition, giving the sense in which they are correctly employed, and a general statement of the principles of electrical science on which the definition is founded. Each of the great classes or divisions of electrical investigation or utilization comes under careful and exhaustive treatment; and while close attention is given to the more settled and hackneyed phraseology of the older branches of work, the newer words and the novel departments they belong to are not less thoroughly handled. Every source of information has been referred to, and while libraries have been ransacked, the note-book of the laboratory and the catalogue of the wareroom have not been forgotten or neglected. So far has the work been carried in respect to the policy of inclusion that the book has been brought down to date by means of an appendix, in which are placed the very newest words, as well as many whose rareness of use had consigned them to obscurity and oblivion.

Copies of this or any other electrical book published will be sent by mail, POSTAGE PREPAID, *to any address in the world, on receipt of price.*

The W. J. Johnston Company, Publishers,
253 BROADWAY, NEW YORK.

ELECTRICITY AND MAGNETISM.

A Series of Advanced Primers.

By EDWIN J. HOUSTON, PH.D. (Princeton).

AUTHOR OF

"A Dictionary of Electrical Words, Terms and Phrases," etc., etc., etc.

Cloth. 306 pages. 116 illustrations. Price, $1.00.

During the Philadelphia Electrical Exhibition of 1884, Professor Houston issued a set of elementary electrical primers for the benefit of the visitors to the exhibition, which attained a wide popularity. During the last ten years, however, the advances in the applications of electricity have been so great and so widespread that the public would no longer be satisfied with instruction in regard to only the most obvious and simple points, and accordingly the author has prepared a set of new primers of a more advanced character as regards matter and extent. The treatment, nevertheless, remains such that they can be easily understood by anyone without a previous knowledge of electricity. Electricians will find these primers of marked interest from their lucid explanations of principles, and the general public will find in them an easily read and agreeable introduction to a fascinating subject. The first volume, as will be seen from the contents, deals with the theory and general aspects of the subject. As no mathematics is used and the explanations are couched in the simplest terms, this volume is an ideal first book from which to obtain the preliminary ideas necessary for the proper understanding of more advanced works.

Copies of this or any other electrical book published will be sent by mail, POSTAGE PREPAID, *to any address in the world, on receipt of price.*

The W. J. Johnston Company, Publishers,
253 BROADWAY, NEW YORK.

The Measurement of Electrical Currents and Other Advanced Primers of Electricity.

By EDWIN J. HOUSTON, PH.D. (Princeton).

AUTHOR OF

"*A Dictionary of Electrical Words, Terms, and Phrases,*" *etc., etc., etc.*

Cloth. 429 pages, 169 illustrations. Price, $1.00.

This volume is the second of Prof. Houston's admirable series of *Advanced Primers of Electricity*, and is devoted to the measurement and practical applications of the electric current. The different sources of electricity are taken up in turn, the apparatus described with reference to commercial forms, and the different systems of distribution explained. The sections on alternating currents will be found a useful introduction to a branch which is daily assuming larger proportions, and which is here treated without the use of mathematics. An excellent feature of this series of primers is the care of statement and logical treatment of the subjects. In this respect there is a marked contrast to most popular treatises, in which only the most simple and merely curious points are given, to the exclusion or subordination of more important ones. The abstracts from standard electrical authors at the end of each primer have in general reference and furnish an extension to some important point in the primer, and at the same time give the reader an introduction to electrical literature. The abstracts have been chosen with care from authoritative professional sources or from treatises of educational value in the various branches.

Copies of this or any other electrical book published will be sent by mail, POSTAGE PREPAID, *to any address in the world, on receipt of price.*

The W. J. Johnston Company, Publishers,
253 BROADWAY, NEW YORK.

THE
ELECTRICAL TRANSMISSION OF INTELLIGENCE,

And Other Advanced Primers of Electricity.

By EDWIN J. HOUSTON, Ph.D. (Princeton).

AUTHOR OF

"*A Dictionary of Electrical Words, Terms and Phrases*," etc., etc., etc.

Cloth.   330 pages, 88 illustrations.   Price, $1.00.

The third and concluding volume of Professor Houston's series of *Advanced Primers of Electricity* is devoted to the telegraph, telephone, and miscellaneous applications of the electric current. In this volume the difficult subjects of multiple and cable telegraphy and electrolysis, as well as the telephone, storage battery, etc., are treated in a manner that enables the beginner to easily grasp the principles, and yet with no sacrifice in completeness of presentation. The electric apparatus for use in houses, such as electric bells, annunciators, thermostats, electric locks, gas-lighting systems, etc., are explained and illustrated. The primer on electro-therapeutics describes the medical coil, and gives instructions for its use, as well as explaining the action of various currents on the human body. The interesting primers on cable telegraphy and on telephony will be appreciated by those who wish to obtain a clear idea of the theory of these attractive branches of electrical science, and a knowledge of the details of the apparatus. Attention is called to the fact that each of the primers in this series is, as far as possible, complete in itself, and that there is no necessary connection between the several volumes.

Copies of this or any other electrical book published will be sent by mail, POSTAGE PREPAID, *to any address in the world, on receipt of price.*

The W. J. Johnston Company, Publishers,
253 BROADWAY, NEW YORK.

ELECTRICITY
One Hundred Years Ago and To-Day.
By EDWIN J. HOUSTON, PH.D. (Princeton).

AUTHOR OF

"A Dictionary of Electrical Words, Terms and Phrases," etc., etc., etc.

Cloth.   179 pages, illustrated.   Price, $1.00.

In tracing the history of electrical science from practically its birth to the present day, the author has, wherever possible, consulted original sources of information. As a result of these researches, several revisions as to the date of discovery of some important principles in electrical science are made necessary. While the compass of the book does not permit of any other than a general treatment of the subject, yet numerous references are given in footnotes, which also in many cases quote the words in which a discovery was first announced to the world, or give more specific information in regard to the subjects mentioned in the main portion of the book. This feature is one of interest and value, for often a clearer idea may be obtained from the words of a discoverer of a phenomenon or principle than is possible through other sources. The work is not a mere catalogue of subjects and dates, nor is it couched in technical language that only appeals to a few. On the contrary, one of its most admirable features is the agreeable style in which the work is written, its philosophical discussion as to the cause and effect of various discoveries, and its personal references to great names in electrical science. Much information as to electrical phenomena may also be obtained from the book, as the author is not satisfied to merely give the history of a discovery, but also adds a concise and clear explanation of it.

Copies of this or any other electrical book published will be sent by mail, POSTAGE PREPAID, *to any address in the world, on receipt of price.*

The W. J. Johnston Company, Publishers,
253 BROADWAY, NEW YORK.

THIRD EDITION

Alternating Currents

—AN—

ANALYTICAL AND GRAPHICAL TREATMENT
FOR STUDENTS AND ENGINEERS.

—BY—

FREDERICK BEDELL, Ph.D., and
A. C. CREHORE, Ph.D., (Cornell University.)

Cloth. 325 pages, 112 Illustrations. Price, $2.50.

The present work is the first book that treats the subject of alternating currents in a connected, logical, and complete manner. The principles are gradually and logically developed from the elementary experiments upon which they are based, and in a manner so clear and simple as to make the book easily read by any one having even a limited knowledge of the mathematics involved. By this method the student becomes familiar with every step of the process of development, and the mysteries usually associated with the theory of alternating currents are found to be rather the result of unsatisfactory treatment than due to any inherent difficulty. The first fourteen chapters contain the analytical development, commencing with circuits containing resistance and self-induction only, resistance and capacity only, and proceeding to more complex circuits containing resistance, self-induction and capacity, and resistance and distributed capacity. A feature is the numerical calculations given as illustrations. The remaining chapters are devoted to the graphical consideration of the same subjects, enabling a reader with little mathematical knowledge to follow the authors, and with extensions to cases that are better treated by the graphical than by the analytical method.

Copies of this or any other electrical book published will be sent by mail, POSTAGE PREPAID, *to any address in the world, on receipt of price.*

The W. J. Johnston Company, Publishers,
253 BROADWAY, NEW YORK.

DYNAMO AND MOTOR BUILDING
FOR AMATEURS.
WITH WORKING DRAWINGS.

By LIEUT. C. D. PARKHURST, U. S. A.

Cloth.   163 pages, 71 illustrations.   Price, $1.00.

One of the most fascinating fields for the amateur is that afforded by electrical science, and the simplicity of construction of small dynamos and motors, in particular, enables him not only to gratify his tastes, but at the same time to construct apparatus that can be directly applied to useful purposes. In Parkhurst's "Dynamo and Motor Building for Amateurs" clear and concise instructions, accompanied by working drawings, are given for the construction of such forms and types of dynamos and motors as are simply made and yet will produce fairly efficient results. While primarily intended for amateurs and students, the detailed information, particularly in the chapters on armature windings, connections, and currents, and on the design of a fifty-light dynamo, will be of value to every electrician. In the latter chapter the subject of the proper proportioning of the armature and armature wire, the calculation of the magnetic circuit and field-windings, etc., are gone into at length, and in the light of the most recent knowledge and practice. The large and clear drawings showing how to wind armatures are supplemented by tables, so that the beginner will have no difficulty whatever in carrying out the instructions. Every part of the machines, even the most simple, is illustrated and marked with its dimensions.

Copies of this or of any electrical book published will be sent by mail, POSTAGE PREPAID, *to any address in the world, on receipt of price.*

The W. J. Johnston Company, Publishers,
253 BROADWAY, NEW YORK.

PUBLICATIONS OF
THE W. J. JOHNSTON COMPANY.

The Electrical World. An Illustrated Weekly Review of Current Progress in Electricity and its Practical Applications. Annual subscription.............. $3.00

The Electric Railway Gazette. An Illustrated Bi-monthly Record of Electric Railway Practice and Development. Annual subscription................ 1.00

Johnston's Electrical and Street Railway Directory. Containing Lists of Central Electric Light Stations, Isolated Plants, Electric Mining Plants, Street Railway Companies—Electric, Horse and Cable—with detailed information regarding each ; also Lists of Electrical and Street Railway Manufacturers and Dealers, Electricians, etc. Published annually.... .... 5.00

The Telegraph in America. By Jas. D. Reid. 894 royal octavo pages, handsomely illustrated. Russia, 7.00

Dictionary of Electrical Words, Terms and Phrases. By Edwin J. Houston, Ph.D. Third edition. Greatly enlarged. 667 double column octavo pages, 582 illustrations..................... 5.00

The Electric Motor and Its Applications. By T. C. Martin and Jos. Wetzler. With an appendix on the Development of the Electric Motor since 1888, by Dr. Louis Bell. 315 pages, 353 illustrations.......... 3.00

The Electric Railway in Theory and Practice. The First Systematic Treatise on the Electric Railway. By O. T. Crosby and Dr. Louis Bell. Second edition, revised and enlarged. 416 pages, 183 illustrations.................................. 2.50

Alternating Currents. An Analytical and Graphical Treatment for Students and Engineers. By Frederick Bedell, Ph.D., and Albert C. Crehore, Ph.D. Second edition. 325 pages, 112 illustrations.................. 2.50

Publications of the W. J. JOHNSTON COMPANY.

Gerard's Electricity. With chapters by Dr. Louis Duncan, C. P. Steinmetz, A. E. Kennelly and Dr. Cary T. Hutchinson. Translated under the direction of Dr. Louis Duncan.................................... $2.50

The Theory and Calculation of Alternating-Current Phenomena. By Charles Proteus Steinmetz 2.50

Central Station Bookkeeping. With Suggested Forms. By H. A. Foster........................... 2.50

Continuous Current Dynamos and Motors. An Elementary Treatise for Students. By Frank P. Cox, B. S. 271 pages, 83 illustrations................ 2.00

Electricity at the Paris Exposition of 1889. By Carl Hering. 250 pages, 62 illustrations. 2.00

Electric Lighting Specifications for the use of Engineers and Architects. Second edition, entirely rewritten. By E. A. Merrill. 213 pages.............. 1.50

The Quadruplex. By Wm. Maver, Jr., and Minor M. Davis. With Chapters on Dynamo-Electric Machines in Relation to the Quadruplex, Telegraph Repeaters, the Wheatstone Automatic Telegraph, etc. 126 pages, 63 illustrations... 1.50

The Elements of Static Electricity, with Full Descriptions of the Holtz and Topler Machines. By Philip Atkinson, Ph.D. Second edition. 228 pages, 64 illustrations..................................... 1.50

Lightning Flashes. A Volume of Short, Bright and Crisp Electrical Stories and Sketches. 160 pages, copiously illustrated............................... 1.50

A Practical Treatise on Lightning Protection. By H. W. Spang. 180 pages, 28 illustrations, 1.50

Publications of the W. J. JOHNSTON COMPANY

Electric Street Railways. By E. J. Houston, Ph.D. and A. E. Kennelly, D.Sc. (Electro-Technical Series)... $1.00

Electric Telephony. By E. J. Houston, Ph.D. and A. E. Kennelly, D.Sc. (Electro-Technical Series).. 1.00

Electric Telegraphy. By E. J. Houston, Ph.D. and A. E. Kennelly, D.Sc. (Electro-Technical Series).. 1.00

Alternating Currents of Electricity. Their Generation, Measurement, Distribution and Application. Authorized American Edition. By Gisbert Kapp. 164 pages, 37 illustrations and two plates 1.00

Recent Progress in Electric Railways. Being a Summary of Current Advance in Electric Railway Construction, Operation, Systems, Machinery, Appliances, etc. Compiled by Carl Hering. 386 pages, 110 illustrations............................. 1.00

Original Papers on Dynamo Machinery and Allied Subjects. Authorized American Edition. By John Hopkinson, F.R.S. 249 pages, 90 illustrations.. 1.00

Davis' Standard Tables for Electric Wiremen. With Instructions for Wiremen and Linemen, Rules for Safe Wiring and Useful Formulæ and Data. Fourth edition. Revised by W. D. Weaver........... 1.00

Universal Wiring Computer, for Determining the Sizes of Wires for Incandescent Electric Lamp Leads, and for Distribution in General Without Calculation, with Some Notes on Wiring and a Set of Auxiliary Tables. By Carl Hering. 44 pages... .... 1.00

Publications of the W. J. JOHNSTON COMPANY.

Electricity and Magnetism. Being a Series of Advanced Primers. By Edwin J. Houston, Ph.D. 306 pages, 116 illustrations............................ $1.00

Electrical Measurements and Other Advanced Primers of Electricity. By Edwin J. Houston, Ph.D. 429 pages, 169 illustrations........ 1.00

The Electrical Transmission of Intelligence and Other Advanced Primers of Electricity. By Edwin J. Houston, Ph.D. 330 pages, 88 illustrations............................ 1.00

Electricity One Hundred Years Ago and To-day. By Edwin J. Houston, Ph.D. 179 pages, illustrated 1.00

Alternating Electric Currents. By E. J. Houston, Ph.D. and A. E. Kennelly, D.Sc. (Electro-Technical Series)................................... 1.00

Electric Heating. By E. J. Houston, Ph.D. and A. E. Kennelly, D.Sc. (Electro-Technical Series)...... 1.00

Electromagnetism. By E. J. Houston, Ph.D. and A. E. Kennelly, D.Sc. (Electro-Technical Series)...... 1.00

Electro-Therapeutics. By E. J. Houston, Ph.D. and A. E. Kennelly, D.Sc. (Electro-Technical Series).. 1.00

Electric Arc Lighting. By E. J. Houston, Ph.D. and A. E. Kennelly, D.Sc. (Electro-Technical Series).. 1.00

Electric Incandescent Lighting. By E. J. Houston, Ph.D. and A. E. Kennelly, D.Sc. (Electro-Technical Series)............................ .... 1.00

Electric Motors. By E. J. Houston, Ph.D. and A. E. Kennelly, D.Sc. (Electro-Technical Series)......... 1.00

Publications of the W. J. JOHNSTON COMPANY.

Experiments With Alternating Currents of High Potential and High Frequency. By Nikola Tesla. 146 pages, 30 illustrations.......... $1.00

Lectures on the Electro-Magnet. Authorized American Edition. By Prof. Silvanus P. Thompson. 287 pages, 75 illustrations........................... 1.00

Dynamo and Motor Building for Amateurs. With Working Drawings. By Lieutenant C. D. Parkhurst... 1.00

Reference Book of Tables and Formulæ for Electric Street Railway Engineers. By E. A. Merrill....................................... 1.00

Practical Information for Telephonists. By T. D. Lockwood. 192 pages.................... 1.00

Wheeler's Chart of Wire Gauges........... 1.00

A Practical Treatise on Lightning Conductors. By H. W. Spang. 48 pages, 10 illustrations. .75

Proceedings of the National Conference of Electricians. 300 pages, 23 illustrations.......... .75

Wired Love ; A Romance of Dots and Dashes. 256 pages.. .75

Tables of Equivalents of Units of Measurement. By Carl Hering......................... .50

Copies of any of the above books or of any other electrical book published, will be sent by mail, POSTAGE PREPAID, *to any address in the world on receipt of price.*

THE W. J. JOHNSTON COMPANY,
253 BROADWAY, NEW YORK.

THE PIONEER ELECTRICAL JOURNAL OF AMERICA.

Read Wherever the English Language is Spoken.

The Electrical World

Is the largest, most handsomely illustrated, and most widely circulated electrical journal in the world.

It should be read not only by every ambitious electrician anxious to rise in his profession, but by every intelligent American.

It is noted for its ability, enterprise, independence and honesty. For thoroughness, candor and progressive spirit it stands in the foremost rank of special journalism.

Always abreast of the times, its treatment of everything relating to the practical and scientific development of electrical knowledge is comprehensive and authoritative. Among its many features is a weekly *Digest of Current Technical Electrical Literature*, which gives a complete *résumé* of current original contributions to electrical literature appearing in other journals the world over.

Subscription { including postage in the U. S., Canada, or Mexico, } **$3 a Year.**

May be ordered of any Newsdealer at 10 cents a week.

Cloth Binders for THE ELECTRICAL WORLD postpaid, $1.00.

The W. J. Johnston Company, Publishers,
253 BROADWAY, NEW YORK.

www.ingramcontent.com/pod-product-compliance
Lightning Source LLC
Chambersburg PA
CBHW030426300426
44112CB00009B/874